Thanawin Ratametha
Manasa Veeragandam

CRM: Software as a Service versus On-premise - benefits and drawbacks

Thanawin Ratametha
Manasa Veeragandam

CRM: Software as a Service versus On-premise - benefits and drawbacks

CRM: Software as a Service versus On-premise - benefits and drawbacks

Lambert Academic Publishing

Impressum/Imprint (nur für Deutschland/ only for Germany)
Bibliografische Information der Deutschen Nationalbibliothek: Die Deutsche Nationalbibliothek verzeichnet diese Publikation in der Deutschen Nationalbibliografie; detaillierte bibliografische Daten sind im Internet über http://dnb.d-nb.de abrufbar.
Alle in diesem Buch genannten Marken und Produktnamen unterliegen warenzeichen-, marken- oder patentrechtlichem Schutz bzw. sind Warenzeichen oder eingetragene Warenzeichen der jeweiligen Inhaber. Die Wiedergabe von Marken, Produktnamen, Gebrauchsnamen, Handelsnamen, Warenbezeichnungen u.s.w. in diesem Werk berechtigt auch ohne besondere Kennzeichnung nicht zu der Annahme, dass solche Namen im Sinne der Warenzeichen- und Markenschutzgesetzgebung als frei zu betrachten wären und daher von jedermann benutzt werden dürften.

Verlag: Lambert Academic Publishing AG & Co. KG
Theodor-Heuss-Ring 26, 50668 Köln, Deutschland
Telefon +49 681 3720-310, Telefax +49 681 3720-3109, Email: info@lap-publishing.com

Herstellung in Deutschland:
Schaltungsdienst Lange o.H.G., Zehrensdorfer Str. 11, 12277 Berlin, Deutschland
Books on Demand GmbH, Gutenbergring 53, 22848 Norderstedt, Deutschland
Reha GmbH, Dudweiler Landstr. 99, 66123 Saarbrücken, Deutschland
ISBN: 978-3-8383-0806-7

Imprint (only for USA, GB)
Bibliographic information published by the Deutsche Nationalbibliothek: The Deutsche Nationalbibliothek lists this publication in the Deutsche Nationalbibliografie; detailed bibliographic data are available in the Internet at http://dnb.d-nb.de.
Any brand names and product names mentioned in this book are subject to trademark, brand or patent protection and are trademarks or registered trademarks of their respective holders. The use of brand names, product names, common names, trade names, product descriptions etc. even without
a particular marking in this works is in no way to be construed to mean that such names may be regarded as unrestricted in respect of trademark and brand protection legislation and could thus be used by anyone.

Publisher:
Lambert Academic Publishing AG & Co. KG
Theodor-Heuss-Ring 26, 50668 Köln, Germany
Phone +49 681 3720-310, Fax +49 681 3720-3109, Email: info@lap-publishing.com

Copyright © 2008 Lambert Academic Publishing AG & Co. KG and licensors
All rights reserved. Saarbrücken 2008

Produced in USA and UK by:
Lightning Source Inc., 1246 Heil Quaker Blvd., La Vergne, TN 37086, USA
Lightning Source UK Ltd., Chapter House, Pitfield, Kiln Farm, Milton Keynes, MK11 3LW, GB
BookSurge, 7290 B. Investment Drive, North Charleston, SC 29418, USA
ISBN: 978-3-8383-0806-7

Abstract

Nowadays, most of organizations try to find the best solution to improve their business processes by using advantage of technologies, which are always developing to replace the mistake of traditional version, one of the most critical evolutions in technology system is Customer relationship management (CRM). CRM stakeholders who implementing CRM system or plan to implement CRM system had faced a lot of uncertainty in new technology, in this case, our focus is on CRM as a Service solution.

CRM as a Service is CRM system that applied software as a service (SaaS) technology as a concept of cloud computing. It is a web-based application that hosted CRM application in provider's side, where clients can access to one copy of application by web browser through internet. To investigate the improvement of CRM, we tried to evaluate SaaS's benefits and drawbacks that assume to affect CRM as a Service solution.

During this process, we had adopted interview as our research methodology and to observe the improvement of CRM system certain to conduct a survey questionnaire. Our research model will be oriented towards investigation of CRM as a Service system based on SaaS's benefits and drawbacks.

In this thesis, we are trying to acquire a better understand in benefits and drawbacks of CRM as a Service which applying the SaaS platform to improve CRM performance, it is helpful to evaluate the CRM as a Service in SaaS's benefits and drawbacks aspects by considering the CRM experts perspective, it help the IT investors in organization, who plan or approach to on-demand service, to gain more knowledge in CRM on-demand service, and in long run to make right decision in CRM solution to their companies.

Key words: Customer Relationship Management, CRM as a Service, CRM on-demand, Cloud computing, Software as a Service, On-demand software, SaaS's benefits and drawbacks, CRM as a Service's benefits and drawbacks.

Authors: Thanawin Ratametha and Manasa Veeragandham

Acknowledgements

We would like to thank the following people is different ways have been support during my master thesis and who have been contributed to the completion of this thesis.

First of all we want to thank our supervisor Erik Wallin for supervising us with patience and guiding us to reach to this point. Thank you for your generous attitude and for sharing your expert knowledge in cloud computing concept and for looking on the bright side when things went completely wrong.

We thank all the members of the companies we visited for the interview for our survey. We are grate full for their time and patience for cooperating with us and for the feedback.

We thank our friends Rajesh, Vini, Ramesh, Gopi for advising us the standards of thesis writing and for being means of encouragement and support.

Last but not least we would pay our sincere gratitude to our family who are solely responsible for bringing us to this standard, who have been great support until this moment of life and who will continue to be the same.

Lund University, June 2009

Authors: Thanawin Ratametha and Manasa Veeragandham

Table of Contents

Abstract 1
Acknowledgements.. ii
Table of Contents.. iii
List of Figures v
List of Tables v
1. Introduction 1
   1.1. Background..1
   1.2. Problem area 1
   1.3. Problem of stakeholders..2
   1.4. Problem complexity 3
   1.5. Research purpose and objective..3
   1.6. Research question 3
   1.7. Delimitation 3
   1.8. Summary...4
2. Related concepts: CRM, Cloud computing, SaaS 5
   2.1. Customer Relationship Management (CRM) 5
   2.1.1. CRM systems 6
   2.2. CRM evolution..7
   2.2.1. Electronic Customer Relationship Management (e-CRM).............................8
   2.3. Cloud computing...9
   2.3.1 Cloud computing movement...9
   2.4. Software as a Service (SaaS) 10
   2.5. CRM on-demand...10
   2.5.1 CRM on-demand services...11
   2.6. Summary...12
3. Theoretical Work 13
   3.1. E-business Model..13
   3.2. Outsourcing CRM system...14
   3.3. Cloud computing concept and SaaS platform...14
   3.4. CRM system to on-demand service 16
   3.5. Impact of SaaS on CRM system 17
   3.5.1. The Pros and Cons of SaaS 18
   3.6. Current CRM implementation status 19
   3.7. Early study in SaaS's benefits and drawbacks..19
   3.8. Summary...21
4. Model about Benefits and Drawbacks 23
   4.1. Summarize key benefits and drawbacks of SaaS..23
   4.2. Evaluate benefits and drawbacks of SaaS...25
   4.3. Research model...28
   4.4. Summary...28
5. Methodology 29
   5.1. Overview...29
   5.2. Interview...30
   5.2.1. Type of interview and Unit of analysis...30
   5.2.2. Design of interview methodology...30

5.2.3. Ethical issues during interview 33
5.3. Online survey questionnaires 34
5.4. Data Presentation 35
5.5. Validating and Reliability 36
5.6. Empirical Work 37
5.6.1. Pilot test 37
5.6.2. Interview 38
5.6.3. Online survey questionnaire 38
5.6.4. Sampling and List of organizations, experts involved 39
5.7. Summary 41
6. Results and Analysis 42
6.1. Interview results and analysis 42
6.2. Survey questionnaire results and analysis 50
6.3. Summary 54
7. Discussion and Conclusion 55
7.1. Discussion 55
7.1.1. Investigation of Software as a Service in CRM 55
7.1.2. Evaluation and validation 56
7.1.3. Challenges and limitations 58
7.2. Conclusions 59
7.2.1. Methodology conclusion 59
7.2.2. Research Conclusion 59
7.3. Suggestion for further R&D 61
7.4. Future work 62
Appendix A: CRM on-demand providers 63
A.1: Saleforce.com 63
A.2: Siebel Systems (Oracle) 63
A.3: Microsoft Dynamic CRM 64
A.4: B2bCRM 65
Appendix B: Interviews 66
B.1: Interview questions 66
B.2: Interview transcriptions 67
Appendix C: Survey questionnaire 79
C.1: www.surveygizmo.com 79
C.2: Online survey Question 79
References 84

List of Figures

Figure 3-1 Overview of Cloud computing platform, SaaS, and e-business model (by authors) 15
Figure 3-2 Impact of on-demand in business model (by authors) 17
Figure 4-1 Research model (by authors)...28
Figure 6-1 Graphical of respondents' opinion in key benefits (by authors)................51
Figure 6-2 Graphical of respondents' opinion in key drawbacks (by authors)............52
Figure 6-3 Graphical of respondents' opinion in comparison of CRM on-demand and CRM on-premise (by authors) 54
Figure 7-1 Adopted procedure for validation (by Guba and Lincoln)........................57

List of Tables

Table 3-1 Summary of literature reviews in SaaS's benefits and drawbacks..............21
Table 4-1 Summary of key benefits and drawbacks in research 25
Table 6-1 Summary of survey questionnaire result in key benefits.............................50
Table 6-2 Summary of survey questionnaire result in key drawbacks 51
Table 6-3 Summary of ranking in key benefits 53
Table 6-4 Summary of ranking in key drawbacks 53

1. Introduction

1.1. Background

Currently, technology has become never ending, new technology always developed to replace the old technology, where organizations can benefit from new ICT (information communication technology) solutions to improve their business processes. Technologies had been changing rapidly, investigation of technology are required in order to choose appropriate technology for their own needs. In this evolution of technology, CRM system itself had developed through time, based on history, CRM is the system that is designed to improve the relation between customers and companies in the long term. In this traditional way, CRM system carried out with face-to-face or telephone transaction, but when age of Internet had reached, most of CRM application had moved online in order to get high efficient to fulfill customers' need called "Electronic CRM" (e-CRM), to which customer can access to CRM application through internet. Unfortunately, it is not stopping at e-CRM, technologies have been developing to fulfill the CRM system, until now, cloud computing concept is the most fashionable platform where software on-demand thoughts is based on cloud computing idea, and this is where CRM as a Service or CRM on-demand established. CRM as a Service is the system that host CRM application into providers' side which is cared by providers. Based on current situation in software on-demand, most of the people had found the benefits from this platform such as cost reduction, low up-front cost, and low implementation, but in other hand, software on-demand also have weakness in itself, such as integration, security, and reliability, which create doubts in investors who decide to move their CRM application into cloud.

In this research, our purpose is to investigate CRM as a Service solution; it will be evaluated in order to demonstrate software as a service (SaaS) platform. CRM as a Service is effected by cloud computing concept where it incorporates with software as a service platform to improve CRM system in offering aspect, more about this effect will be explained in this report later. With this objective, we are going to investigate CRM as a Service solution, which is applied form of SaaS platform in CRM system. By doing this, key benefits and drawbacks of SaaS that are assumed to be affecting the CRM system will be indicated based on previous researches, and we will conduct research methodology for evaluating those key benefits and drawbacks by empirical study through interview and survey questionnaire method. But first of all, we would like to illustrate background of the topic and problem space of this research which we are going to investigate in order to create good understanding about this topic for a depth investigation process in further chapter.

1.2. Problem area

First of all, we would like to introduce our research problem area to create well understand and scope problem area into our research interest. In this research, our problem area focuses on CRM as a Service solution where investigation will accomplish in this area. But first we would like to mention about our main problem area which is CRM system. These days, CRM system is growing very fast, evaluation of CRM system keeps changing. Companies always look for suitable technology for their business process. SaaS is one of the interesting technology that still questioned by CRM stakeholders, as we known that SaaS can improve their CRM system implementation, but it still need evaluation in this technology based on their affection to CRM system. IT investors and others interested in making the case for IT investment must situate more attention on this investigation, where benefits and drawbacks of SaaS that affect to CRM system will be evaluated in order to use make right decision in CRM solution that fit to their organization. Moreover, CRM on-demand also provides misery in this problem, CRM as a Service can benefit organization and improve the CRM system compared with traditional on-premise CRM. But most of the customers still have doubt on CRM as a Service capability and how can it benefit their business opportunity. Customers still ask question about "Is it secure enough?", "Is it reliable enough", "Does it make financial sense?" and the common question is "Should they upgrade their CRM system to host application or not?" (Preston, 2008).

Ultimately, CRM as a service can benefit organizations but in other hand, it also can harm organization with its drawbacks. Choosing new CRM system depends on load of factors of organization. To gain best profit, discussion and evaluation about this technology has to be a concern. Moreover, SaaS platform claims as disruptive technology (Chou, 2008), time and research are needed to evaluate advantages and disadvantages. However, conducting this research will give better understanding in CRM as a Service for CRM stakeholders. Besides, in order to investigate CRM on-demand benefits and drawbacks, it will be referred to traditional on-premise CRM system to compare the improvement between both systems in SaaS's benefits and drawbacks aspect. At the end, information will be gathered from empirical study and conclude as a useful knowledge for decision in IT investment.

1.3. Problem of stakeholders

According to our research problem area, as we know that SaaS can improve their CRM implementation, but still need more evaluation of this technology based on their benefits and drawbacks. This problematic has effected to all CRM stakeholders, which can divide into 2 main affected groups which are consumers and providers.

In consumers' aspect, it includes Companies that implement CRM system or plan to implement new CRM system, organization IT investors, and decision makers in organization. These groups of stakeholders were suffering in unstable and misery of CRM on-demand solution, and they are not certain to implement CRM on-demand for their organization. They must change the term of the discussion by focusing on benefits and drawbacks of CRM on-demand solution that consider in ability to fit CRM on-demand to their organization business processes or not. In other hand, for providers' aspect, it includes the vendors that provide quality of services, and experienced implementers in CRM system. Based on subscription model, providers attempt to claim that on-demand solution is the best; the doubts are still remaining to on-hosted CRM. To get rid of these problems, providers should indicate key benefits and drawbacks that affect the CRM on-demand solution, and evaluate it to show advantage and disadvantage for customers' choices, and try to eliminate weakness of their products.

1.4. Problem complexity

At present, there are many CRM on-demand vendors; most of them claim that they can benefit their customers in many ways. But, there are no exact explanation that how SaaS improve CRM system also with SaaS's drawbacks. There are some previous articles mentioned about SaaS benefits and challenges, but they are not strong enough to conclude everything in one way. Additionally, SaaS platform in CRM system is still young technology where cloud computing concept is not solid to large size of application. The rate of adoption for SaaS is moving steadily ahead, but the delivery mode has not been universally accepted. Based on Aberdeen Group survey (Aberdeen.com), 3 of 4 companies planning to implement on-demand application in next two years, but 42 percent of that had no plans to implement within these two years (Judith, 2009). Most organization still not certain about SaaS application, rarely knowledge in SaaS platform is obstruction during the decision making process.

1.5. Research purpose and objective

Our research purpose is to investigate CRM as a Service solution when applied SaaS platform to improve efficient of CRM system. By doing this, key benefits and drawbacks of SaaS that consider as effect to CRM system will be indicated and evaluated. In this case, our objective is to identify the benefits and drawbacks of SaaS that affect to CRM as a Service, comparison between CRM on-demand and traditional CRM on-premise will be conducted based on its benefits and drawbacks proposition. Additionally, based on CRM revolution in last decade, we found that it shows trends of CRM implementation that mostly focus on e-business implementation. During research process, each key benefit and drawback will be evaluated based on improvement of CRM on-demand solution based on real CRM implementation life cycle in order to gain exact information from the real world.

1.6. Research question

Based on our research purpose and objective, we tried to investigate the improvement of CRM as a Service which applied SaaS platform to CRM system. By doing this, we will evaluate the key benefits and drawbacks that concerned to effect to CRM as a Service solution. Our main research question will be based on:

- How Software as a Service can improve the CRM system?
- How benefits and drawbacks of SaaS affect CRM using Software as a Service compared with traditional on-premise CRM?

Each key factor will be divided into two categories; benefit and drawback, and build as main research model in order to evaluate CRM as a Service in empirical world to answer main research question above.

1.7. Delimitation

As we had mentioned that, CRM as a Service can benefit organization in many aspects but it also can create weakness in their system. In this research, to investigate CRM as a Service solution, our delimitation is based on key benefits and drawbacks of SaaS that believe to affect to CRM system, it will indicate and evaluated as main idea in our research model. To do so, in order to study the improvement of CRM system with SaaS platform, key benefits and drawbacks were evaluated based on enhancement between CRM on-demand and traditional CRM on-premise. Moreover, we have selected Customer Relationship Management (CRM) module in ERP system as our research interest area. Because of, CRM systems facilitate organizations to track and manage their customer relations; according to e-business model offering, CRM system is mostly applied into e-business solution called "e-CRM", to advance and improve offering level in CRM service model (Hedman & Kalling, 2002). Recently, CRM system is most trendy to use as Software as a Service platform in last few year (Weier & Smith, 2007), the idea is to apply SaaS concept to CRM system and turn everything to on-hosted software application. In this case, we focus on benefits and drawbacks of SaaS that assume to effect use of CRM as a Service solution.

1.8. Summary

We have introduced our research background and have given little detail about our research area in this concept and have mentioned about the problem area in which we are doing in our research, also stakeholders who involved with this problem was defined, where complexity of research problem was concerned. Then, research purpose had indicated based on our problem area and we will be illuminating the research questions for further investigation. CRM system implementation is complex, and it often fails during its process. CRM failures have been costly, disruptive, and discomforting to organization. Careful evaluation and understanding is required in order to decide about implementation. Our research objective is to compare traditional CRM and CRM as a services solution based on SaaS's benefits and drawbacks and sees how SaaS benefits the CRM system implementation. Besides, SaaS platform has benefit for organizations, but on the other hand, it can also affect the organizations with its drawbacks. Choosing between traditional CRM and CRM as a service depends on the number of factors of organization. To obtain best profit, evaluation of benefits and drawbacks is required, in addition, SaaS platform is a disruptive technology; time and research need to evaluate advantage and disadvantage to make verification on this technology.

2. Related concepts: CRM, Cloud computing, SaaS

In this chapter, related concepts will be mentioned, which describe detail of the object of study. Start with, introduction of CRM and its definition will be dealt where functionality of CRM system will be defined. Next, evolution of CRM will come up, also the definition of e-CRM system. Moreover, cloud computing movement will be introduced as a new trend for business process, where software as a service is defined as a new software platform that effect from cloud computing movement. At the end of chapter CRM on-demand will be introduced as a result of applied software as a service platform into CRM system, and service of CRM on-demand is to be acknowledged.

2.1. Customer Relationship Management (CRM)

The customer relationship management (CRM) system is an enterprise system that helps organization to manage customer relationships in a structured way. It is a way of using technology that consists of the processes a company uses to track and organize its contacts with its current and future customers. CRM system can manage relationship between customers and organizations in effective way. The CRM software is used in the processes of the customers' information and their interactions can be entered, stored, and accessed by the employees in different departments of the organization. The goal of CRM software is to improve the services that are provided to the customers and by using their customers' information to targeted marketing. Moreover, in the integration aspect, company can benefit from shared information to other department where all information of the customer is stored in the central system (Hedman & Kalling, 2002).

With CRM technology services, CRM offering two main types of service as on-premise (internal hosted application) and on-demand (through Software as a Service (SaaS). Moreover, CRM operation includes many aspects however we personally found the most significant aspect should be defined by Kabiraj as author stated the CRM as below.

- *"Front office operations: operation between customers and organization. For example, direct contact to customer via email.*
- *Back office operations: this operation occurred inside organization which effect to front office operation. For example, marketing plan.*
- *Business relationships: to create the strong relation between customer and organization by interacting with third parties such as vendors or suppliers.*
- *Analysis: using CRM information to analyze the data into valuable knowledge in order to benefit organization in business aspect"* (Kabiraj, 2003, pp. 484).

CRM has wide aspects as it could be front office operation, back office operation etc. Ultimately, the significant of CRM is these 4 aspects, which are undoubtedly utilized by an organization in order to develop the relation between customer and those organizations.

Basically, CRM can support the interaction between customers and organization which create strong relation between those stakes, analyzed data will use by other business sections to complete their business requirement, such as using for planning marketing strategies. In addition, Hedman and Kalling stated "CRM system" that

"... are designed to improve the understanding of the customers and the market and, in the long term, to improve a firm's market position and profitability. The customer preferences, competitors, emerging competing business models, relation with the customers, and function of the offering and all other important aspects pertaining to the market can be well analyzed through CRM systems." (Hedman & Kalling, 2002, pp. 156-157)

For this state, the essential of CRM is obviously not for the stakeholder but also the other business sections will benefit from this system by using analyzed data through CRM system. Due to applying into the business model, Hedman and Kalling found that in those three layers; offering, activities and organization and resources could be improved the efficiency by applying CRM. Basically, CRM has several proposes for improved business such as develops business strategy etc. Ultimately the core of CRM intends is described by the same authors as above

"...the objectives of CRM systems should be ... to enable collaboration between people working within a business model or between business models..." (Hedman & Kalling, 2002, pp.157)

Personally, we agree with Hedman and Kalling that the collaboration is key of CRM as it deliver channel to customer in order to keep strong relation between stakeholders and also the benefits of organization might gained from integration system in order to apply the data. In addition, information will be accessible through the organization, which means that the customer will gain this information in order to have continuous response.

2.1.1. CRM systems
CRM system is the system that used for collecting and maintaining customers and competitors data, and providing tools to analyze including the report for business objective, where customer insight of the offering perception. Function of CRM system is to process and collect vast amount of customer data and use of that information to fulfill the business model. Customer information will effect to resources layer such as sales, marketing, etc, offering (price and cost), and the activities and organization of the business model. Mostly CRM system is based on

open and flexible technologies, for instance database, TCP/IP, and XML (Hedman & Kalling, 2002).

In addition, CRM system consisted of 2 main parts, first is software and data-processing logic, which are core function of determine and process the data; second part is databases and hardware, where those data was stored. But with CRM components, CRM consisted of a lot of components depend on type of works and business requirement. Hedman and Kalling stated some of the components as following;

- *"An opportunity management component*
- *A configuration component*
- *A partner relationship component*
- *An interactive selling component*
- *A call center component*
- *An analysis component*
- *A campaign management component"* (Hedman & Kalling, 2002, pp. 159-160)

From this state, we have seen that CRM in each organization, it is rather various due to CRM itself not necessary has to have all components, it depends on CRM could possibly match to solve the business problem and its functionality.

2.2. CRM evolution

As we mentioned that Customer Relationship Management (CRM) system is our research interest. CRM systems facilitate organization to track and manage their customer relations; it is mostly applied into e-business solution such as Application Service Provider (ASP) called "e-CRM". Recently, based on Cloud computing concept movement, CRM systems are most fashionably used as Software as a Service platform in last few years (Weier & Smith, 2007).

Dickie mentioned CRM evolution by focusing on sales aspect; author stated that the initial focus of CRM applications was relation between sellers and buyers. However, over the past few years, that have been changing; more functionality had developed to support the sales process in CRM system. Some vendors offer advance tools that providing analysis feature to utilize what salespeople need to complete their business, such as more effectively detail products, improve cross-selling and up selling, and etc (Dickie J., 2004).

Moreover, last decade, on-demand computing explodes onto the CRM scene. It was a certified as disruptive innovation that would change the way we think about software and how we use it (Chou, 2008). This decade, the technology has certainly lived up to its advance billing but, remarkably, it has not resulted in the end of software as we know it. Besides, CRM system also developed to catch up the new technology during these periods, to improve the efficiency of CRM system implementation, new technologies were applied to advance CRM system. Cloud computing was applied in order to improve and fulfill CRM system, move from traditional (on-premise) system to Software as a Service (on-demand) is one of solution that effect from cloud computing movement, which it expected to improve CRM system in cost, implementation aspect, etc.

2.2.1. Electronic Customer Relationship Management (e-CRM)

The new generalized form of CRM is called Electronic customer relationship management (e-CRM). E-CRM facilitates the growth of relationship marketing strategies that consider on obtaining a better understanding of customers' need. The strategy of e-CRM is that it gives an understanding that how the customers wants to do the business with the firm in the long run but not how the firm want to do the business with the customer. Also nowadays, most of the companies use internet to increase the efficiency of their business strategy, also with usage of internet customer relationship was improved (Johnson, 2002). This made CRM vendors to provide them improved capabilities by introducing to e-CRM. As there is huge growth of the Internet, CRM vendors provided application service online for customers which allow customers to access into same features and functions at the same time. Jukic and author's colleagues stated that e-CRM is combination between CRM and internet; it uses benefit of internet to increase the efficiency of CRM. E-CRM can simply deliver to customers by using internet web-browsers. By doing this, organization can send information into target customers directly; also can create tough relation with customers by providing exactly what customers' need (Jukic et al, 2003). The e-CRM allows the customers of the companies to access the company services from more places as the internet service is huge in the usage of mobile, e-CRM is the further step that allows the customers to access the system through mobiles phones with internet access or PDA (Camponovo et al, 2005).

Nowadays, internet is most important factor to success in business process; most of organization concern that internet can benefit their business process in many aspects, for example, it can reduce customer-service costs, create strong relation between customers and organization. But most important aspect is that it can enable mass customization in CRM process which can offer products and services to individual customers based on their particular need (Johnson, 2002). Also, with the support of Sales Force Automation (SFA), electronic methods were applied to gather and analyze customer information automatically, use of internet and SFA can seen as foundation of movement from normal CRM to e-CRM. We can define e-CRM as activities to manage customer relationships by using the internet, web browsers or other electronic devices. Main advantage of e-CRM is to offer right information and communication to right customers' needs, also offer controllability to customer in order to customize their information through internet (Jukic et al, 2003).

Moreover, e-CRM providing new channel that allow companies to communicate with their customers in easier way, as a result, more attention and time was gained from customers. The reason that make e-CRM are very popular is that, it not only transaction for customers but it can provide unique and positive experiences to them by using advantage of internet through web-browser (Wind & Mahajan, 2002). According to e-CRM character, it is highly interactive character, where customers can response to their needs immediately through digital channel, which can help companies to keep strong relation in long-term customer relationships (Winer, 2001).

2.3. Cloud computing

Based on Gartner analysis group defined cloud computing style that it is a concept of IT computing which provide advance capability to scale the IT potential through the service by using advantage of internet to offering service to multiple customers at the same time and same application (Gartner report, 2008). By perception of offering, cloud computing provide business service application online through application interface accessed by web browser, where software application and data was stored in the external server. The cloud computing has essential underneath the local computer due to all the data and applications will be kept in server. Hence, it is not only to decrease the work load into personal computer but also for the user own sake as well. For this reason, only access to internet and click on web browser, then your system will be handled by expert.

Moreover, Williams and Sears (2008) as well as Campbell (2008) show that there are many technologies that are created on cloud computing concept, such as Infrastructure as a Service (IaaS), platform as a Service (PaaS), and Software as a Service (SaaS), it shown the effect of using internet to create new opportunity to offer new kind of services to organization (Williams & Sears, 2008)(Campbell, 2008). Additionally, cloud computing is the main concept of using benefit of internet to create strong network infrastructure, in order to improve the way of delivery data and application (Scanlon & Wieners, 1999).

2.3.1 Cloud computing movement

While talking about CRM as a Service, we can relate to Software as a Service (SaaS) platform, and above all of these concept, let start with cloud computing concept, it play important role as a key framework for these days online service. Cloud computing is the main key theoretical in our research; it is style of computing that offer dynamically activities including effective resources as a service over the internet (Gruman & Knorr, 2008). By doing this, users need not have knowledge expertise or control skill over the technology infrastructure "in the cloud" that supports them. Next, the concept of cloud computing incorporated with Software as a Service (SaaS) trends that create theme of trust on the internet for fulfilling the computing needs of the users (Campbell, 2008). Nowadays, most of providers turn themselves into cloud by providing on-demand application as a new channel of service delivery, where application and data of clients stored on external server and client can accessed through internet.

From the beginning, everything started from Cloud computing; it is the next step in information technology. Researchers studied on cloud computing concept, which is about secure, reliable, financial sense, etc. As InformationWeek analytics cloud computing reports that, most of organizations still have doubt on moving into cloud, and they not yet decide to move their IT infrastructure into cloud computing platform (InformationWeek report). But nowadays, based on rapid grow of marketing and business competition; organization need to achieve their business opportunity and offer to their customers. SaaS platform was established to serve this situation by its defined benefits such as fast implementation, low cost and price, easy to deployment and management.

2.4. Software as a Service (SaaS)

Software as a Service (SaaS) is an application hosted on a remote server and accessed through the Internet. Nowadays, web 2.0 is being widely use in the internet, it begin with small application such as email, photo, etc, until now, software application services online start to deliver through web browser. Moving to web-based application create huge change in methodologies and way of working (Google Docs). Yet, Fred stated that SaaS is one type of application based on web 2.0 or cloud computing concept, it offer the service through web-browser to a lot of customers in one time by using multitenant architecture (Fred, 2009). Moreover, on customer aspect, SaaS benefit customers by decreasing up-front cost and software licensing, in the other hand, due to provider aspect with SaaS platform, there is only one application to maintain which is much lower cost compared with traditional application (Fred, 2009). Nowadays, SaaS is the accepted platform that provide common delivery model as basic technology to deliver service to clients, it is supported by web service and service-oriented architecture (SOA) such as Asynchronous JavaScript and XML (Ajax), and even broadband service has become increasingly available to support user access from more areas around the world. It is also called as Web-based software or On-demand software.

Madsen stated SaaS that it is a delivery method that providing accessibility to customers by subscription-based model via internet (Madsen, 2009). Meanwhile, internet service have become more popular in order to support user access from everywhere around the world, also with the rapidly grow of web service solution in e-market to support user's need. Based on SaaS characteristic, SaaS concept is related to Application Service Provider (ASP) and on-demand computing software delivery models. In ASP, providers give accessibility for users to access to available software which delivers it over the internet website. But in software on-demand computing, it is related with SaaS concept, where providers offering customers network-based access to a single copy of an application.

SaaS is one of interesting solution that provides benefits to improve quality of CRM implementation or call "CRM as a service" or "Hosted CRM". With SaaS delivery model, it provides ability for business processes to gain benefit from new technology with low and clear initial cost. Currently SaaS is the most interesting software platform and useful in order to lower Total Cost of Ownership (TCO) and visible return of investment cost (Software & Information Industry Association [SIIA], 2004).

2.5. CRM on-demand

CRM as a Service or CRM on-demand or on-hosted CRM (it has gone by various names) is CRM system that applied SaaS platform by providing CRM application service through the internet sites which can be accessed by internet browser. As we mentioned, in order to fulfill the rapid change of customers requirement and high competition in the market, SaaS platform can serve up as key concept to survive in current high competition market. CRM as a Service can benefit organization in many ways such as improve implementation speed, low cost of investment (Anthes, 2009). Moreover, On-demand software also benefits some financial advantages over applications installed and supported behind the firewall (Finch, 2006), but many of the other advantages push by its follower have disappear. For example, CRM on-demand software was initially easier to implement, but that was when the applications were relatively simple. On the other hand, even though CRM on-demand has a many advantages, but it also have some disadvantages in itself such as security, integration with legacy systems, control of application and data (Weier & Smith, 2007). Since its start, CRM on-demand has raised a lot of questions from CRM practitioners. Most of service vendors start to providing CRM on-demand services in recent years, but traditional on-premise CRM still remain as alternative for customers. Nowadays, most of organizations pay more attention in on-demand service, CRM as a Service should be evaluating based on its benefit and drawbacks that effect to the organization's business process which can use those knowledge to support decision-making process in CRM investment.

2.5.1 CRM on-demand services

CRM system have developed to catch up the new technology during these periods, to improve the efficiency of CRM system implementation, new technologies were applied to advance CRM system, move to Software as a Service (SaaS) is one of solution, which expected to improve CRM system in many aspects such as cost, implementation, and etc.

Nowadays, on-demand trends are very fashionable in CRM field with the result of cloud computing concept and SaaS platform. CRM on-demand or hosted CRM is CRM system that applied SaaS platform to benefits the CRM system which create innovative way as software is delivered as a service through the internet. CRM on-demand system hosted in providers' side where providers will response for everything, users can remotely access the system through internet browser without any installed software client. Additionally, hosted simply means someone else is managing the application on a computer that is remote from the user. At present, most of CRM providers launch their new on-demand services to customers, most of famous on-demand providers are Saleforce.com[1], it is the biggest provider in CRM on-demand (Pring, 2005), Oracle also have Siebal[2] CRM on-demand, also big company like Microsoft had sent Microsoft Dynamic CRM[3] in the market, and so on. CRM on-demand market was growing rapidly, and there is high competition in on-demand market. Most of CRM on-demand service providers claim that they are the best solution and their customers can get benefit from CRM on-demand solution. But on the other hand, some customer might not be sure about this technology and fear in new technology. At this point our research will investigate CRM as a Service, and its benefits and drawbacks in order to verify this unsteady technology.

---

[1] See appendix A, A.1 for Saleforce.com information
[2] See appendix A, A.2 for Siebel system information
[3] See appendix A, A.3 for Microsoft Dynamic CRM information

2.6. Summary

The CRM is defined, it is a way of using technology that consists of the processes a company uses to track and organize its contacts with its current and future customers. It includes many aspects front office operations, back office operations, business relationships, analysis. CRM systems and it evolution has been described and other related topics to CRM are also defined in this chapter as follow, Electronic Customer Relationship Management (e-CRM), Cloud Computing, Software as Service (SaaS), CRM on demand. With "e" generation, it is new generalized form of CRM is called Electronic customer relationship management (e-CRM). CRM systems facilitate organization to track and manage their customer relations; it is mostly applied into e-business solution such as ASP called "e-CRM". Recently, CRM system is most fashionably used as Software as a Service platform influenced by cloud computing. The cloud computing is a style of computing which is dynamically scalable and often virtualized resources are provided as a service over the Internet. Users need not have knowledge, skill, or control over the technology infrastructure in the cloud. From the beginning, everything is started from cloud computing; it is the next step in technologies evolution. Based on cloud computing and its movement, this concept is incorporate with SaaS platform, Gartner report defined cloud computing as a style of computing where extremely scalable IT-related potential are provided as a service using internet technologies to multiple external customers (Gartner report, 2008). Besides, CRM system also developed to catch up the new technology during these periods, to improve the efficiency of CRM system implementation, new technologies were applied to advance CRM system; move to SaaS is one of solution, which expected to improve CRM system in cost, implementation, and etc. SaaS is an application hosted on a remote server and accessed through the internet. It create new solution of CRM system called CRM on-demand, it is CRM system that applied SaaS platform by providing CRM application service through the internet sites, which can be accessed by internet browser. Nowadays, vendors start to turn themselves into cloud and providing CRM as a Service solution to their customers, for example, biggest on-demand vendors is Salesforce.com who providing full service of CRM on-demand solution.

3. Theoretical Work

In the last chapter, we have introduced important concept that related to our research area. In this chapter, theoretical work is reviewed in order to organize research structure as empirical investigation procedure. Beginning with e-business model theory; this is the main theory to explain the cloud computing concept and SaaS platform. Another theory is outsourcing of CRM system, to describe evolution of CRM system to on-demand service. Also, affection of SaaS will describe in order to explain how SaaS effect to CRM system based on pros and cons of SaaS. Then current CRM implementation status will be evaluated, and at the end, the early study in SaaS benefits and drawbacks in the last few years will be reviewed to build research model in next chapter.

3.1. E-business Model

Coming in era of networked economy, internet is widely used to create new firms and new business model in order to improve their business capability. New terms and concepts were establishing from the networked economy era, most of the popular used term is "e-business". In 1997, IBM company is first used term e-business in their campaign, since then, "e" term was used widely in businesses such as e-auction, e-banking, and e-commerce. According to "e" evolution, most of companies try to survive in high competitive market in long run, they were adapted to their business process from traditional business model to e-business model by developed in technologies like Transmission Control Protocol/Internet Protocol (TCP/IP) and Extensible Markup Language (XML). Additionally, e-business model is the idea that uses benefits of internet to advance traditional business model capability. Also, some important advantage of internet usage is, it can expand market reach, visibility, responsiveness from customers, new feature and channel of services, and cost reduction (Hedman & Kalling, 2002).

The designing of an e-business model is important in the process of information system development in the area of e-commerce as a key to develop business routine to success case. According to Hichem and Wahiba, operating the e-business strategy of a company by the utilization of the technology in the value created for the company itself and its business partners is the reason for the design of an e-business model (Hichem & Wahiba, 2005). E-business strategy can define as process of creating customers' value by using benefit of technology, in this case, using utility of internet. By the implementation of Web solutions, e-business model supports the e-business strategy and the value chain activities of the company for value creation in the favor of the company and its partners. Thus, e-business modeling is concerned with degree the intra organizational integration activities, layout of the client interface, position of the company in the business network in the industry value chain.

Moreover, Gordjin and Akkermans stated that, in order to success in implementing e-business model in organization, there is lack of management aspects in IT perspective which is not sufficient to business perspective. Thus in order to gain benefit from an e-business, the integration of these two perspectives must be done. In the e-business environment, it is easier for the new elements to be added or removed to the business chains when compared to the traditional business. Thus when illustrating an e-business model, it is important to state the exchange between the particular elements (Gordjin & Akkermans, 2001). E-business models have chance to improve the relationships with the customers by exploiting the opportunities that are provided by the ICT, which is a characteristic that differentiate them from the traditional business models (Hichem & Wahiba, 2005).

3.2. Outsourcing CRM system

Hedman and Kalling (2002) defined three theories that are valid in explaining the cause of outsourcing: transaction cost theory, the research-based view and the institutional theory of organization (Hedman & Kalling, 2002). Based on these three theories, outsourcing in CRM system also explains by using three of these theories. Why outsourcing CRM, first, according to transaction cost theory, firm outsource because the overall cost external production is lower than the overall cost of internal production. Nowadays, most of the organizations realize that outsourcing CRM system cost lower than implementing by internal IT resource. Next, resource-based explanation, firms outsource IT in order to support their core business processes, and free up their IT internal resource, this is another reason that why most of companies outsourcing their CRM system, and they don't need to worry about their CRM system and can focus into their core business with full capacity. Also, it can free up internal IT resource in their organization which can get rid of hidden cost in organization. Last theories that use to explain is Institutional theory, decision-making is affected by individual norms and values and by identity, based on current treads of CRM system, outsourcing is one of the fashionable choice in CRM implementation, that's why most of company try to outsource their CRM system, even it not improve the financial result of the company. The above reasons can use to support why most companies choose to outsource their CRM system in order to advance their customer relationship management offering and move themselves into cloud, which are the effect of applied e-business model into CRM system.

3.3. Cloud computing concept and SaaS platform

Based on e-business model, Hedman and Kalling presenting the components of e-business model as eight components which are customer value, scope, price of the offering, sources of revenue, connected activities, implementation, capabilities, and sustainability (Hedman & Kalling, 2002). Cloud computing concept was applied to the e-business model as theoretical framework in order to offer the new age of internet services. As we mentioned, cloud computing also related to eight components of e-business models, cloud computing offering distinctive and lower cost solution for customers who are willing to use on-hosted services through internet sites, providers or vendors will charges customers for accessibility to services site. Moreover, on-hosted service offering low risk implementation and no need of expertise skills during implement period. IT internal resource is no more needed and activities in organization will be affected in better ways. Above benefits of cloud computing, can be explained by e-business model which are improved features of traditional business model.

Software as a Service (SaaS) is one of the technologies that incorporate to cloud computing concept. SaaS is the on-hosted or on-demand software/application services through internet sites. According to industrial organization-based framework of

Applegate (as cited in Hedman & Kalling, 2002), it used to explain how SaaS platform affects to organization structure and business model. SaaS defined as new business market opportunity, and the new software services offered. Its concept has effect to organization structure, culture, operating model, infrastructure model, etc. Moreover, SaaS platform can create value in business model by improving efficiency of offering level.

Moreover, Software as a Service (SaaS) had applied e-business model to offer better solution to improve the cost and price. According to "Generic of e-business model" of Rappa (as cited in Hedman & Kalling, 2002), *"Subscription model was applied as main idea to improve the business models in software service provider to the level of offering on business model."* Based on its definition, subscription model users pay for access to the site or services, SaaS platform used subscription model to create benefit in business model by using e-business model concept, it is offering general strategy in low cost software services for customers (subscribers). In figure 3-1, it shown overview relation of how cloud computing, SaaS, and e-business model relate together.

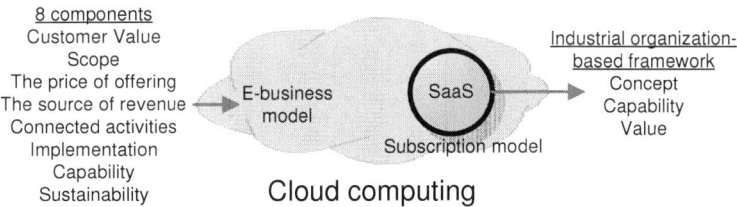

Figure 3-1 Overview of Cloud computing platform, SaaS, and e-business model (by authors)

Due to evolution of CRM system in fully integration aspect to increase efficiency of business model, it is the effect from parallel development of technology which creates improvement in CRM system, especially the internet. According to Payne et al., perhaps writing prior to the real emergence of e-CRM, detail a business model which stresses the need for marketing as a "cross functional activity" across departments. It is essential aspect behind;

"this brings greater flexibility due to its integration, helping it to achieve better "quality, service levels, cycle times" via newly established "pools of resources"; not simply finance or marketing but a "market facing team" offering all functions of the business to the consumer." (Payne et al., 1998)

Based on this stated, integration between IT and other business sections become core concept of CRM system in order to improve offering layer in business model. Moreover, Handen (as cited in Brown, 2000), suggests that technology has improved the process in three core areas: *"the Internet, in work flow management, and through data warehousing"*. And these three advancements used to support cross organization department in integration aspect (Payne et al., 1998).

Nowadays, CRM system is the most fashionable system that always implement as e-business model. At a time of economic uncertainty, there are decreasing amount of money in CRM system investment, most of companies put more focus on cost-reduction aspect rather than increase revenue by finding new customers. The challenge to the business line managers who own customer care strategies is to avoid complete CRM displacement. In these circumstances, while building the business case for CRM projects, managers need to concentrate on projects that quickly demonstrate returns that play to the economic requirement of retaining customers and reducing costs. Moreover, with the low up-front costs and fast deployment period of SaaS, it can create opportunity to focusing on customer experience in application, which constructs strong relation to customers. And it is the reason why CRM system is most fashionable application in applied SaaS platform (Weier & Smith, 2007).

3.4. CRM system to on-demand service

In order to improve relation between customers and organization efficiency, CRM systems had been applied into organization to create increase marketing opportunity and advance firm's market position. There are attempts to improve CRM business model in order to create efficient in CRM system. According to effect of e-business on the business models, Hedman and Kalling stated that in offering level, offerings are the focus of e-business models. They could even be called offering models. All e-business models include offerings, and some include several offerings. Subscription model is considered in this level. They describe

"...traditional businesses have adapted e-businesses to fit their own business models. This has improved the cost and price of offerings in most industries. New tools have been developed and used to investigate and survey customer's perception of e-business models and offerings." (Hedman & Kalling, 2002, pp. 232)

Based on effect of e-business model on the business models, CRM system had effect on the business model in every level, starting with resources, the offering, activities and organization and, finally, the market. But in this case, key point is offering level, the offering (products or services) and the perception of the offering are affected by adopting a CRM system, which ultimately will affect price, cost and profit. How CRM systems affect the price, cost and profit of a firm depends on the actual use of system. In this sense, to improve CRM system offering, e-business model was applied with CRM system (e-CRM) to improve the offering level in business model. CRM on-demand is CRM system that applied SaaS platform (on-hosted) to advance CRM system service, as we mentioned, SaaS platform use subscription model to improve business model in offering level, in this case, CRM on-demand also benefit its business model in offering level by this theory, in figure 3-2 shown how CRM on-demand impact on business model.

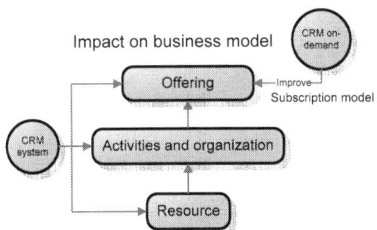

Figure 3-2 Impact of on-demand in business model (by authors)

The movement of CRM system to hosted software can benefit the organization in many ways, in order to investigate CRM on-demand's benefits and drawbacks, referring to traditional CRM (on-premise CRM) will require, comparison between advantage and disadvantage of both systems to demonstrate the improve of CRM system with SaaS platform (CRM as a Service). CRM stakeholders need good understanding about difference between on-demand and on-premise CRM system, in order to choose right solution that suit for their organization, and decision making is based on each advantage and disadvantage of each service type of CRM system.

3.5. Impact of SaaS on CRM system

As we mentioned that, SaaS is subset of Cloud computing concept, SaaS use cloud computing concept to create new service opportunity through internet website. According to SaaS characteristics, SaaS is a web-based service by using subscription model, in technological aspect all the responsibility is in vendors' hand. At the theoretical aspect, in SaaS the users has to do only accessing; first the end users are getting Web access and then the vendor is getting paid. However, software-as-service (SaaS) has essential agenda as it should imply as 'secret weapon' in order to reduce work load in clients, as Reid stated that core of SaaS is to offering greater operation efficiency, low costs, and shared resources among clients (Reid, 2009).

Next, as we have identified that CRM on-demand or hosted CRM is CRM system that applied SaaS platform to improve offering level in business model. Based on its definition, CRM on-demand solutions are delivery of Sale Force Automation (SFA) and apply service on browser. However at the beginning of first launch had failed due to the variety of reasons, then, the developed generation, it is rather success as its point not being second-class due to it could possibly decrease cost of ownership. Ultimately, even the CRM is constantly improving in the business, yet it might not be steadily provided to all vendors (Borck, 2005).

According to CRM on-demand vendors' competition, Oracle is challenging Salesforce.com's lead in CRM as a Service with a need release of its CRM on demand. In doing so, Oracle offering more features and functionality in deployment options than Salesforce, also offering lower monthly cost per user than Salesforce does which make Oracle to become better option for CRM users (Weier, 2009). In this case, we can see high competition between providers in CRM on-demand market, to which most of provider try to focus on main benefits of CRM on-demand like cost reduction or offering in functionality, and make themselves become leader in CRM on-demand providers. This is just an example of CRM as a Service provider competition, according to CRM on-demand trends, most of CRM vendors try to capture benefits of SaaS platform, and provide new CRM on-demand solution to fulfill their customers' requirement.

3.5.1. The Pros and Cons of SaaS

As we mentioned that SaaS is outstanding option in adopting IT business infrastructure to the cloud computing platform. But somehow, not every business process is suitable for this technology (Hall, 2009). SaaS can benefit to IT business infrastructure, but other hand, there are some weakness of SaaS that we should concern as threat to this technology. To choose between on-premise and on-demand, investor should have good understanding about its advantages and disadvantages of SaaS should consider in order making sure that this technology suite to their business processes.

Madsen (2009) stated about advantages of SaaS that compared with on-premises software, SaaS benefits in low initial cost and predict monthly cost, and with low initial fee rate, it can increase speed of implementation too. Also author mentioned that because of SaaS software is maintained and upgraded by providers, users can get rid of installing and upgrade problem and they can focus on their core business process (Madsen, 2009). Moreover, Hall also mentioned that SaaS is cost-effective model, top of the reason that why customers choose SaaS is the cost, where SaaS provide ability to predict and manage about cost to users (Hall, 2009).

Although SaaS has many advantages, the investors also concerned about the disadvantages of SaaS. As Madsen mentioned that customization is one of the most important disadvantages of SaaS, if customers' business process is complicated and need lot of customization and configuration, they shouldn't pick SaaS to be their software platform. Even though, most of providers claim that they can configure screen for personal usage, but somehow, be sure that customization is possible. Furthermore, integration and security were stated by Madsen, about integration aspect, author mentioned that it is great challenge in SaaS to integrate internal system with hosted application on internet. Another disadvantage is security, author stated that security is main issues to choose between on-premise and on-demand platform, because of SaaS is multi-tenancy system, where multi people can access into one copy of application which storage in same database, author questioned that *"did software secure enough to display only owner's data?"* (Madsen, 2009).

Additionally, Hall said that SaaS is a "risk-reward model" which means that it can benefit core business of customers but you take a risk to put core business process outside company (Hall, 2009). Weighting between pros or cons of SaaS should be done carefully, there are application and organization that perfect fit to SaaS platform, but some situation, organization prefer to run their business in-house. Madsen also stated that mostly it will depend on nature of application and users, need of integration system, and IT policy in security aspect (Madsen, 2009). Above pros and cons of SaaS is main issues during the implementation, in this research, we try to indicate all possible benefits and drawbacks of SaaS based on literature review which shown in further topic.

3.6. Current CRM implementation status

Based on nature of CRM implementation, CRM implementation is complicated and numerous time and money were consumed to complete the project. Some of projects might face the failure situation; also most of CRM projects can't follow exactly the same business processes as organization's requirement.

According to previous research about Implementation complexity, Martin stated that *"scope control of implementation will be more difficult than expected and the level of outside expertise required will be higher than anticipated."* (Martin, 1998). These obstructions cause CRM implementation project fail or late more often, without good plan and control. There are some attempts to increase the value of their CRM initiatives while keeping costs low (Ledford, 2004). But suitable strategies will be different for every organization; companies need to go back to basics for reducing costs and to increase ROI (Return Of Investment). These basic strategies defining clear CRM strategies, change management, and budget management. They are most important details in making CRM initiatives successful, ensuring long-term ROI, and increase implementation successes.

Moreover, Adebanjo mentioned that to success in e-CRM implementation, it is depend on good management strategies since the beginning of the process, but somehow, there is no exact guideline to lead to successful way (Adebanjo, 2008). Hopefully, Software as a Service is suitable technology for mentioned basic strategies in order to benefit e-CRM system which can reduce cost and visible return of investment cost. But now, it needs evaluation to investigate this technology's benefits and drawbacks and to improve the implementation of CRM on-demand solution.

3.7. Early study in SaaS's benefits and drawbacks

According to early study in SaaS benefits and drawbacks, we had found loads of articles which are related to our interest and we try to summarize those articles based on its key concern about benefits and drawbacks of SaaS.

In year 2005, Dubie (2005) stated that, with on-demand software, organization can implement specific application expertise with low implementation initial cost and low implementation and investment risk. But in other hand, it can cause the problem in integration with other systems; customize the application, and security problem (Dubie, 2005). This 2005 was the early year in this study, we found that the main benefit of SaaS was low upfront investment and low implementation risk and also the drawbacks of SaaS was integration problem with legacy system, due to it was newly technology.

In 2006, Finch (2006) mentioned about several benefits of SaaS model, including low cost of entry, responsibility is on the vendor, less risky investment, cost prediction, and flexibility to change usage commitments as business circumstances change. Unfortunately, author didn't mention about drawbacks in this article (Finch, 2006).

In 2007, Weier and Smith (2007) had mentioned about adopting SaaS referring to its benefits and drawbacks, they concerned about the benefits including ease of deployment and management, lower cost, not locked into long license, and predictable software costs. Also concerned with the reason that why isn't adopting SaaS, which are security, reliability, features and functionality, and integration with legacy system (Weier & Smith, 2007).

During the year 2008, people start turn their interest to SaaS platform, many articles mentioned about its advantage and disadvantage, concerned about SaaS's benefits and drawbacks was raised. According to Weier (2008), author mentioned that the low up-front costs of CRM services get the most attention; the real test of success will be quickly integrated with all parts of a business. The challenges of integrating CRM on-demand with on-premises IT systems remains a barrier to adoption, and CRM as a Service vendors are clamoring to prove they have the most flexible platform (Weier, 2008b). Then Stimpson (2008) had found that with unreliable of bandwidth and security problems of online services, most of organization still hold themselves to move to hosted applications (Stimpson, 2008). Moreover, Fonseca was concerned about SaaS drawbacks in *"SaaS Benefits Starting to Outweigh Risks"* which include security, control of application and data, integrating with legacy problems, and customization problems (Fonseca, 2008). Further, Lashar (2008) was concern about hidden cost of SaaS, author said that *"The value proposition is well known by now: solid functionality that can be implemented quickly with low costs. But just how low are those costs? Do the economics withstand examination?"* (Lashar, 2008). Besides, Matt (2008) reviewed the advantage of SaaS in article *"The Sales Force Software Shift"*; author had mentioned 9 pros that make SaaS benefits organization (Matt, 2008). Additionally, Biddick (2008) was concern about issues that related to cloud computing concept and SaaS platform, according to the survey security is the most concerned issue, control, vendor lock-in, and configurability respectively (Biddick, 2008).

In year 2009, Anthes (2009) had studied in SaaS realities, author concerned about hidden costs and security issues, where choosing new IT services needs to concern about budget and business demands (Anthes, 2009). Next, Lager (2009) mentioned about cost reduction, author stated that with strongest point of CRM on-demand is to reduction in cost when compared with tradition (Lager, 2009).

Above summary of some articles that have strong relation to our research interest, based on literature reviews, summarize of SaaS's benefits and a drawback from year 2005 to 2009 is shown in table 3-1.

Table 3-1 Summary of literature reviews in SaaS's benefits and drawbacks

Year	Benefits	Drawbacks
2005	• Low implementation and investment risk • High and fast ROI	• Integration • Customization • Security
2006	• Low cost of entry • Responsibility is on the vendor • Less risky investment • Cost prediction • Flexibility to change usage commitments as business circumstances change	
2007	• Ease of deployment and management • Lower cost • Not locked into long license • Predictable software costs	• Security • Reliability • Features and Functionality • Integration with legacy system
2008	• Low upfront costs and IT initial costs • Mobility • Ease of deployment and management • No need IT infrastructure • Low cost and price (Total cost of ownership) • Fast implementation • Low implementation and investment risk • New functionality and improved application performance (flexibility) • High and fast ROI	• Integration • Customization and Configuration • Security • Control of application and data • Lack of flexibility, offering, features and functionality • Lack of application development and enhancement • Connectivity • Cultural different • Low CRM benefits • Reliability and connectivity • Vendor lock-in and long term vendor commitment
2009	• Get solution up quickly • Low IT initial • Fast implementation • Cost reduction • No need to build IT infrastructure or expand IT staff	• Security • Vendor lock-in • Customization

After we had summarized all key benefits and drawbacks from previous researches, in next chapter, we will decide on key factors that assume to affect the CRM on-demand solution. Evaluation in each key factor will be described in order to construct our research model as the purpose of this research.

3.8. Summary

In this chapter we have evaluated the theoretical work for the empirical data for our research work. The designing of an e-business model is important in information system for the development of e-commerce as a key to develop the business routine. In the concept of Cloud computing and SaaS, it were applied to the e-business model as theoretical framework in order to offer the new age of internet services and it can related to eight components of e-business model mentioned by Hedman and Kalling. SaaS is on-hosted or on-demand software/application services through internet sites and explains how SaaS platform affects to the organization and business model. It offers better solution to e-business model to propose solution to improve the cost and price. In outsourcing the CRM systems, it is explained by defining the three theories by Hedman and Kalling, based on those three concepts it is explained the cause for outsourcing CRM systems. Moreover, SaaS use cloud computing concept to create new service opportunity through internet website. A brief description is given on SaaS by explaining through its pros and cons. There are attempts to improve CRM business model in order to create efficient in CRM system by using subscription-based model. This is well described in the CRM System to On-demand service. Our research is based on the benefits and drawbacks of SaaS that affect to CRM system, according to previous researches about benefits and drawbacks of SaaS, all important factors have been listed by year. And it will indicate and evaluate in next chapter in order to constructing as our research model of investigation.

4. Model about Benefits and Drawbacks

In the last chapter, we mentioned early study in SaaS benefits and drawbacks. In this chapter, the summary of key benefits and drawbacks were reviewed and evaluated. Then, our research model is build based on those key benefits and drawbacks, which will use as main idea in empirical investigation.

4.1. Summarize key benefits and drawbacks of SaaS

Since we summarize all early studies in term of SaaS's benefits and drawbacks, therefore in this part we will decide on the key benefits and drawbacks that has strong concerned by SaaS's stakeholders. In order to summarize and select the key benefits and drawbacks, we consider issues concerned with the benefits and drawbacks of SaaS in year 2005 to 2009[4]. Hence, we will explain each benefit and drawback in detail, and summarize them into our research key benefits and drawbacks for further evaluation in CRM as a Service.

According to SaaS's benefits, there is no doubt that SaaS can reduce the cost and price including reduce total cost of ownership during the implementation period, this stands one of the important benefit. Preston said that subscribing own application to vendors service is cheaper than implementing whole on-premise system, also author stated that, with subscription model, customers need not pay up-front costs for IT infrastructure, just pay for the usage (Preston, 2008).

Since low up-front costs and low IT initial in implementation, it can create higher and faster in return of investment (ROI). Moreover, SaaS provide ability to new functionality and improved application performance during the period which create more flexibility in implementation (Dubie, 2005)(Wallach, 2008).

Instead of paying lots of money to roll out a complex solution across the entire company, customers can complete their CRM system with small amount of IT internal resource, also, with the small investment if it fails, the risk will be accepted. Moreover, SaaS vendors provide customer's flexibility to change usage commitments in the case of unstableness of business circumstances also will be motivated to fix the problem (Finch, 2006).

In addition, SaaS provide ability to predict the cost with the clear subscription-based model, and can get rid of vendor lock-in problem in long license contract, also benefits in ease of deployment and management during the implementation period (Weier & Smith, 2007). Moreover, with the great benefits of SaaS, it is the ability to get solution so quickly and do not have to build out infrastructure or expand IT staffs (Anthes, 2009). Another benefit is mobility, SaaS platform can access it anywhere through internet browser, from a PC in the office to a laptop (Stimpson, 2008)(Hewitt, 2008).

---

[4] See chapter 3; 3.7, Table 3.1

Although SaaS can benefit organization in many ways, it also has weakness in itself. Security is one of the important issues to be concerned in SaaS; many larger companies for a long time avoided hosted services because of concerns about security (Fonseca, 2008). Customers still concerned about the security with the question in their mind that *"Is data held somewhere in the cloud and piped over the internet as secure as data protected in enterprise-controlled repositories and networks"* (Preston, 2008).

Even integration is one of the main issues between licensed and hosted software, vendors should find the best solution to fit their customers' business process in integration aspect (Dubie, 2005). In addition, Weier stated that integration problem remain barrier to on-demand adoption, but in the same way, most of the vendors claim that they can get rid of this problem with their flexible integrating interface platform (Weier, 2008a).

With customization and configuration aspect, based on subscription model, SaaS is multitenant application where many people access into one copy of application, on-demand vendor should provide ability to customize and configure application without effecting to the application source code for any individual customer. Customizing and configuring aspect in SaaS platform need good concern to create value and to fit with customers' business processes (Sun et. al, 2008).

Besides, Fonseca had concerned about controllability on application and data, author said that most of the customers feel sore to host their confidential application and data outside their organization (Fonseca, 2008). Moreover, concern with connectivity and reliability, as we mentioned that on-demand application can access via internet, where connectivity and reliability is not sufficient by customers. Stimpson said that vendors should provide capacity to test with clients' connectivity to determine level of speed and reliability to be sufficient by customers (Stimpson, 2008).

Moreover, Preston said *"How easily could I pick up my application from one vendor and move it to another?"* (Preston, 2008). Vendor lock-in and long term vendor commitment also can cause the problem with customers who are willing to change SaaS providers because of its standards and contrast.

Based on SaaS characterization, it has same application standard and platform which cause the lack of flexibility and offering during implementation. Moreover, features and functionality offering is not enough to suit the customers' particular business processes, more specific development and enhancement of application will be required to fulfill customers' requirement (Weier, 2008b).

Unfortunately, SaaS may actually impede the ability to realize full entitlement to CRM value. The cost is not a direct cost, but rather an opportunity cost in terms of lost CRM benefits, in some case, on-premise CRM system had advantage over CRM on-demand in this aspect (Lashar, 2008).

Ultimately, because hosted solutions can be accessed from anywhere, firms should evaluate the potential impact by allowing employees to work from home and what opportunities exist for hiring remote employees and concerned about culturing impact in this perspective (Stimpson, 2008).

After all, we had summarized all key benefit and drawback based on above explanation, and it result in 12 key benefits and 9 key drawbacks as shown in table 4-1 below.

Table 4-1 Summary of key benefits and drawbacks in research

Benefits – (12)	Drawbacks – (9)
• Low cost and price (Total cost of ownership) • Low up-front costs and IT initial costs • Low implementation and investment risk • Clear cost prediction • Not locked into long license • Ease of deployment and management • Fast implementation • No need IT infrastructure and free up internal resource • Mobility • High and fast ROI • Flexibility to change usage commitments • Responsibility is on the vendor	• Security • Integration • Customization and configuration • Control of application and data • Reliability and connectivity • Vendor lock-in and long term vendor commitment • Lack of flexibility, offering, features and functionality • Low CRM benefits • Culture different

4.2. Evaluate benefits and drawbacks of SaaS

After we had selected key benefits and drawbacks of SaaS from previous research articles, next we will explain in detail for each factor and evaluating each key factors to gain more understand and to create research model to investigate improvement of CRM system by applying SaaS platform as defined in our research objective.

Benefits

Surely that CRM on-demand can reduce cost and price during the implementation; everything will be taken care by vendors including hardware (server, backup server, etc), software maintenance, upgrading and so on. Implementation costs can be 25 percent to 40 percent of on-premise implementation costs in terms of the costs for internal staff and professional services, and there is no cost of IT infrastructure because everything is hosted by vendor (Lashar, 2008). Based on Transaction cost theory in IT outsourcing (Hedman & Kalling, 2002), CRM on-demand considered as outsourcing which can use transaction cost theory to explain the cause of reduction in cost, because outsourcing CRM system is cheaper than in-house implementing their own CRM system. Moreover, with all responsibility is on vendor, during the initial state of implementation, customers don't need to build their own IT infrastructure such as server, storage, etc. As well, there is no investment in IT resource, hardware, and expertise in CRM field, which create low up-front costs and IT initial costs comparing with on-premise CRM system. In this case those customers don't need to invest lot of money to implement CRM system; it causes lower risk in implementation in case that implementation in CRM system is a failure and it is easy to roll back to the implementation project when things don't go right. Based on overall cost reduction of CRM on-demand, customer will have advantage in high and quick return of investment, because they don't invest lot of money during the initial implementation period.

As we mentioned in theoretical framework that, subscription model create more opportunity in offering level in business model, which is new way to deliver the service to customers, and this is one of the strongest point of SaaS benefits. According to CRM on-demand subscription-based model, users pay to access to the site, which create clear picture in expending cost, it allow customers to have clear cost prediction in monthly or annually, because expend cost of customers can calculate in "cost per users" and it is easy to predicting overall cost in future. Additionally, with this advantage of subscription model, customers don't have to locked into long license anymore, comparing with on-premise CRM system, customers have to pay lot of money in license cost and sign the contract in long-term to use the software, but with subscription model, customers pay accessing cost to the provider which is free to locked into long-term of contract in software license. Likewise, it provides customers ability to change usage commitments as business circumstances change by the time. According to rapid change in business requirement and high competition in CRM field, this subscription model present flexibility to adapt the business requirement and it is effortless to change compared to on-premise CRM system that require more time and resource consumption.

Furthermore, with the limited scope of customize and configure the system, it make faster in implementation and create lower up-front cost. As well, implementing system on SaaS platform, companies don't need to manage application and system, which can reduce internal IT staffs in organization. Moreover, on-demand providers offer service on support and upgrade the system with new features and functionality including all other operational services, in this case, customer don't have to take care about these aspects and get rid of hidden cost problem. Based on resource-based explanation in IT outsourcing (Hedman & Kalling, 2002), to outsourcing CRM system into vendor, internal IT staff can focus on their core business during the implementation which do not need to concern about deployment and management problem, and it also can free up internal IT resource in the company because need no expertise in CRM on-demand system. As results, all of these advantages are caused by outsourcing CRM system to vendor, which everything will take by expert's hand. Another benefit of SaaS is Mobility, based on on-hosted software service, CRM on-demand can access by internet sites, which create high mobility in work because CRM on-demand system can access anywhere through personal Notebook, PDA, or any device that can connect to the internet, it is easy to connect and work from everywhere.

Drawbacks
On the other hand, the nine weaknesses that consider as key drawbacks of SaaS that effect to CRM on-demand implementation are evaluating as follow. The biggest issues that seem to be big problem for CRM stakeholders are security. According to hosted software, all data and application of customers will be hosted at vendor server, and vendors will take care for everything. Some customers still have doubt on data and application security because they hosted all data and application in external servers and those might not be safe enough for their confidential data, it still in top of mind for most customers (Preston, 2008), Moreover, same reason that CRM on-demand will be hosted by vendors, customers have concern to the controllability of application and data, which they can't have full control on their own application and data comparing with on-premise CRM system that hosted by internal server. With this issue, customers feel that they have no right on their own application/data and

more time consuming in order to manage their data. Before implementing on-hosted CRM, good question should ask the vendors about security and authority policy, where vendors should provide clear secure and clear policy to make sure that customers data and application is in under control and they have full authority to control their own application and data. Moreover, based on InformationWeek research survey in Weier, author concerned about integration aspect that,

"Integration with non-SaaS apps is the top SaaS challenges (62%) voted by 159 companies who using or planning to use SaaS" (Weier, 2008a)

As results, most of the companies had concerned about integration problem in SaaS, where it is very complicated process to integrate external application with existed internet system. Even through, SaaS platform is very easy to implement and companies prefer to use on-demand because of its simplicity and cost savings, but integration aspect is a biggest obstruction in on-demand implementation. Moreover, as we mentioned that the core functionality of CRM system is to integrate the system to other departments in order to create value in data to fulfill organization needs, but with integration issue in on-demand software, it seems that on-demand technology are not going fine with CRM system.

Even though, SaaS has benefit from the economy scale based on its web-based delivery model to serve services to big amount of customers, but in other hand, SaaS can cause the customization and configuration problem from this benefit. Wei and author's colleagues stated that SaaS platform developed from highly standardized software functionalities which are low flexible in its interface, where many of the clients require more ability to customize and configure their application based on their unique business processes (Wei et al, 2008). From their concern, customers always want to customize and configure their application to best suit their working behavior, where CRM on-demand vendors providing limit of customization and configuration based on their standardized software functionalities. With this reason, that's why, CRM on-demand is not suitable for large scale organizations that require high customization and configuration in their application to suit their complex business model. Moreover, with limited standard software functionalities to serve many of the clients, it also effect on the lack of flexibility in offering the new features and functionality to serve customers' unique business needs. And this can be the big problems in long-run term when customers can't work on their unique and complicate requirement. Another issues that concerned by limited standardize functionalities is low CRM benefits, based on limited scope of features and functionalities, plus low money investment in implementing CRM system, it will reduce usage capacity of CRM system, and customers will not get best benefit from using CRM system comparing traditional CRM system.

Furthermore, based on CRM on-demand sites, customers can only access to their application through internet browser, enough bandwidth and capacity of provider server is required in creating reliable during the work time. Based on Stimpson (2008), author concerned about connectivity issue that *"the biggest issue we've found is making sure that you have a fast and reliable Internet connection?"* In further, Preston was concerned about Vendor lock-in and long term vendor commitment issues, author concerned about internet specification that it is enough reliable to ensure that SaaS platform can provide ability to move their data through the cloud (Preston, 2008). In other words, customers still have the question that how easy to move from one vendor to another vendors when trying to compare with premised-based CRM. And the last key drawbacks is culture different, according to mobility of CRM on-demand, customers can access from anywhere that can connect to the internet, which effect to work behavior of employees in organization, issue in new opportunity of working progress will raise, cultural difference issues need to be concern in order to work in efficient in CRM on-demand system environment.

4.3. Research model

After all, our research model will be demonstrated based on those key benefits and drawbacks. We had selected factors that it often concern as key issues from each category and construct our research model to evaluate CRM on-demand by referring to CRM on-premise system based on those key benefits and drawbacks Then our research model has illustrated to evaluate CRM on-demand based on twelve benefits and nine drawbacks of SaaS that we consider as key issues. To investigate CRM on-demand, each key issue in benefit and drawback will be evaluated by interviewing expertise in CRM field; evaluation will be referred to CRM on-premise in order to estimate improvement of CRM system with SaaS platform. Our research model is shown in figure 4-1 below.

Benefits
- Low cost and price (Total cost of ownership)
- Low up-front costs and IT initial costs
- Low implementation and investment risk
- Clear cost prediction
- Not locked into long license
- Ease of deployment and management
- Fast implementation
- No need IT infrastructure and free up internal resource
- Mobility
- High and fast ROI
- Flexibility to change usage commitments
- Responsibility is on the vendor

Drawbacks
- Security
- Integration
- Customization and configuration
- Control of application and data
- Reliability and connectivity
- Vendor lock-in and long term vendor commitment
- Lack of flexibility, offering, features and functionality
- Low CRM benefits
- Culture different

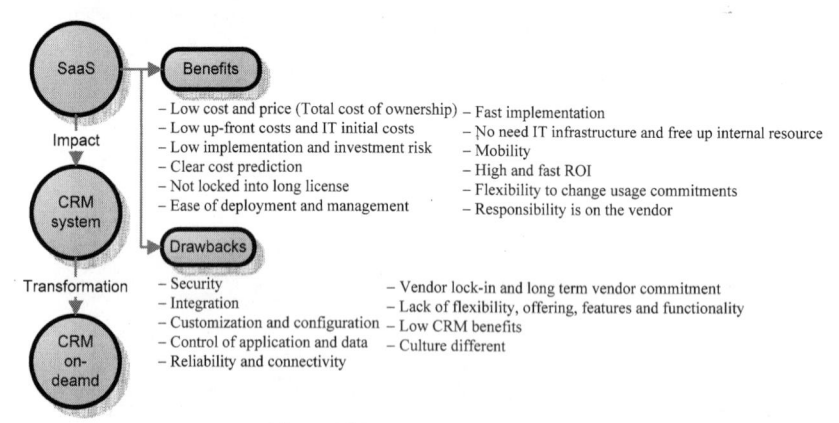

SaaS → Impact → CRM system → Transformation → CRM on-deamd

Figure 4-1 Research model (by authors)

4.4. Summary

In this chapter the key benefits and drawbacks of SaaS has been summarized and evaluated as mentioned in the earlier chapter. Some of the key benefits and drawbacks, which consider as effect to CRM on-demand system, have been evaluated in order to create research model to investigate CRM as a Service solution. Based on these key benefits and drawbacks our research model is constructed and our further investigation is continued for empirical study by research methodologies which explain in next chapter.

5. Methodology

5.1. Overview

In previous chapter, research model was build as investigation tool for the empirical study. This chapter will cover the methodology used in this research. This chapter outlines the research methodology and illustrates the methods used to investigate the research model and thus offer answers to the research problem and research questions. According to our research strategy, Oates (2006) said that a research strategy is overall approach to answer the research question; in this case, we plan to investigate the CRM as a Service by using survey strategy. Survey focuses on achieving the same kind of data from a large group of people, in a standardized and systematic way (Oates, 2006). Based on our research objective, we tried to investigate the improvement of CRM as a Service solution when applied SaaS platform to CRM system, key benefits and drawbacks of SaaS that are considered to affect the CRM as a Service will be indicated and evaluated by using this strategy.

Investigation process design
In order to gather all necessary information, we would apply mixed methods, both Qualitative and Quantitative methods. Due to empirical data should be collected in expertise perspective, therefore the professional aspect from the expertise will be established by the interview method, and for widely perspectives in CRM stakeholders, empirical data will be gathering via survey questionnaire method in order to supporting interview collected data.

After we have generated some data, by using survey strategy and interview with online survey questionnaire data collection, we need to analyze the data by looking for relationships and themes in data. In quantitative data, mathematical approaches will use as tool to analyze and interpret the data. In qualitative data, the analysis is to looking for relation and theme of collected empirical data where it can organize as categories divided by interpreted meaning (Oates, 2006). Moreover, Kvale (1996) said that qualitative and quantitative methods are tools, and their efficiency depends on quality of the empirical study methods.

In this empirical study, interview method will produce qualitative data which can apply qualitative data analysis method; in this case five approaches are used to dig out knowledge. With online survey questionnaire, it will generate quantitative data which can apply statistical approaches to analyze the data and conclude the knowledge to verify interview result. Knowledge will be used to fulfill and support the last conclusion and conclude as one to answer the research questions.

Next we will explain about data collection methods which are interview method and online questionnaire method in detail. After that sampling target group will be mentioned, also with expected result explain about what kind of result we will collect, how can we collect, and how can we analyze them, including how to conducting quality research concerned with ethic issue, validity, and reliability. Then, data presentation will be mentioned in order to explain how to present and interpret the data from our research methodology in efficient way. And last, empirical work will mention where all details in empirical study methods will defined.

5.2. Interview

As we mentioned, we will use interview method to collect the empirical data in our research. According to Oates (2006), author defined the interview that interview is one type of conversation but with careful concern in subject, questions, and answer during the conversation. So these conversations are planned discussion between people. Also, Kvale says those interviews is in structured form and have a purpose for the conversation, where propose of questioning is need to gather the data (Kvale, 1996).

Based on above interview definitions, we decided to conduct the interview in order to investigate benefits and drawbacks of SaaS that affect to CRM as a Service solution. Our plan is to interview CRM on-demand providers who are well experienced or working with CRM on-demand and expertise in this area. Interview questions based on benefits and drawbacks of SaaS will be asked to the participants and our observation will be on their answer and opinion which will be used as information to analyze and conclude as valued knowledge to answer our research questions. To control the interview in scope of our research interest, interview question will be asked based on research model[5]. Next, we will explain our design in interview method in more detail.

5.2.1. Type of interview and Unit of analysis

Based on type of interview, Oates had defined that interview was divided into three types, structured, semi-structured and unstructured interviews, each type have its own specific condition and appropriate way to use it (Oates, 2006, pp. 187-188). In this case, time consuming, inadequate contribution and less experience of interviewer for analyzing the data, "Structured interviews" method will be used. The Interview will be conducted with a script in the form of questions, and there is no flexibility in the order of questions. This is the most structured and efficient way of the qualitative interviewing techniques and is useful for reducing bias when several interviewers are involved, and interviewers are less experienced or knowledgeable, or possible to compare the responses of different respondents.

Our investigation is based on company unit; we plan to interview vendors who are providing CRM on-demand service. Project manager or Team leader is asked to participate in the interview, in order to gain real implementation experience in management level.

5.2.2. Design of interview methodology

Our interview method is based on seven stages of an interview investigation of Kvale which are thematizing, designing, interviewing, transcribing, analyzing, verifying, and reporting (Kvale, 1996).

Thematizing and Designing
The first two stages of an interview study are Thematizing and Designing. Kvale defined Thematizing stage that, it is to create good understanding to investigate

---
[5] See chapter 4; 4.3, Figure 4-1

subject, where reason and explanation in concept of investigation should be investigated before interviews start, "why" and "what" question should be asked before "how" to ask question (Kvale, 1996). Also, author stated that based on designing stage on seven stages of investigation, all stages should be considered before the interview starts, by assuming and planning the whole investigation process for future knowledge.

In thematizing stages, Kvale had stated that the key questions for planning an interview investigation should be what, why, and how of the interview (Kvale, 1996, pp.95). This method originally is the way to the goal, in this research, our Thematizing stage of interview based on Kvale definition, cloud computing and SaaS platform was reviewed, with CRM system, in order to gain pre-knowledge in our research subject. Moreover, our research questions[6] were identified in order to clarify the purpose of the study which is to investigate the benefits and drawbacks of SaaS that affect CRM as a Service solution. Then, interview method was picked as tool for empirical study to analyze and obtain knowledge for further stages.

After the first stage of thematizing an interview investigation by clarifying its content and purpose – the second stage, designing, consists of overall planning and preparing the methodical procedures for obtaining the intended knowledge. Relating to our research design the interview; we had plan to conduct face-to-face interview in companies that are expertise in CRM on-demand field. Good plan and schedule was prepared in order to manage time and money consumption during the interview period. As we had mention that our plan is to interview three CRM on-demand providers which are appropriate number to obtain vary expertise opinion and to balance quality and quantity of interviews. And last, interviewer will conduct the pilot test for set of interview questions and conducting interview simulation for good preparation to obtain quality in interview.

Interview situation
Furthermore, during the interview, Kvale had concern about framing the interview that briefly introduce about interview subject and context should be done before interview start, which interviewer should define interview situation to interviewee, and debrief contexts will be conducted afterward (Kvale, 1996). During the interview, the interviewer will briefly inform about the purpose of the interview, the use of a tape recorder, and the right of interviewee at the beginning of interview. Moreover, further explanation about the interview investigation should preferably wait until the interview is over.

Next, interview guide, to have good and smooth interview period, an interview guide indicates the topics and their sequence in the interview. The guide can contain just some rough topics to be covered or it can be a detailed sequence of carefully worded questions. Refer to our research model in previous chapter, we will conduct the interview based on our research model, questions will be asked by interviewer in sequence following each key benefit and drawback factors in the research model. Our interview question will create based on each key benefit and drawback factor referring to benefits and drawbacks of SaaS that effect to CRM as a Service solution

---

[6] See chapter 1; 1.6

in our research model, for example, with low cost and price benefit, the question will ask that "Did SaaS reduce cost and price (Total Cost of Ownership) of CRM system? Please explain", see appendix B (B.1) for interview questions. Moreover, our research questions will promote a positive interaction; keep the flow of the conversation going and motivate the subjects to talk about their experiences and feelings by using the question like "Please explain", "How?", or "Do you agree with". Furthermore, Kvale mentioned about interview question that Interview proceeds are like normal conversation but with purpose and structure form of questioning. The interviewer's questions should be brief and simple (Kvale, 1996). As we mentioned that structured interview is used in our interview, with set of question and asked in sequence which are designed as simple as possible in order to make clear and understandable question to interviewees.

Conducting qualitative interview
Next, interviewing stage, to conducting the interview, we are concerned about issues of quality in interview research. Kvale said that interview is beginning stage of gathering process which will be used for analysis in further process, the quality of interview is dependent on raw material from the beginning, for which it require professional skills to conduct interview and to have good understanding about interview purpose (Kvale, 1996). In order to launch validity interview result, it should certainly concern at the ground process. Kvale mentioned that based on quality criteria for an interview above, our research interview method is eventually conducted based on these criteria in order to be able to achieve quality in interview as gaining quality of information for further analysis.

Recording interview and Transcription
Before turning to the analysis of the knowledge constructed in the interview interaction, recording interview and transcription method is required during the interview period. This topic addresses the procedures for making interview conversations accessible to analysis which are taping the oral interview interaction by tape recorder, transcribing the tapes into written texts.

Kvale mentioned about recording interview that the method of recording interview conversation for further processes, mostly tape recorder is used as tool to record the interview. By doing this, interviewer can focus on the interview subject during the interview without concern about nothing (Kvale, 1996). During our research interview, we used tape recorder as tool to record oral conversation between interviewer and interviewee, in order to remind and collect every words and interviewer can concentrate on interview subject during the period.

After we taped all conversation, next step is to transcribe into texts. The usual procedure for analyzing is to have the taped interviews transcribed into written texts. Moreover, transcribing the interviews from an oral to a written mode structures, the interview conversations is in an agreeable form for closer analysis. Structuring the material into texts facilitates is in itself a beginning analysis. Researcher will act as transcriber to translate oral taped conversation to text, moreover, transcription is based on same style according to different transcribers, and exactly same word are translated into texts divided by sentences' owner (interviewer and interviewee). Then, transcription is used for further analysis explained in next chapter.

Analysis with "5 approaches"
After converting oral conversation into text; now this is step of analysis by using 5 approaches of analysis. They can be used to organize the interview texts, to condense the meaning into forms that can be presented in a relatively short space, and to work out implicit meanings of what was said. Five main approaches to interview analysis is used: categorization of meaning, condensation of meaning, structuring of meaning through narratives, interpretation of meaning, and ad hoc methods for generating meaning (Kvale, 1996, pp. 192-193).

Five approaches are applied as analysis method in our research; first all the transcribed text is condensed and filter into shorter and meaningful formula. Next, we divided text into categories based on our key benefits and drawbacks in research model. After we divided into category, we narrowed the structure to bring out its meaning based on stories told during an interview, by doing this, we rearranged the structure of category into meaningful way in order to interpret the meaning for a text to answer our sub research question (in each key factors). At the end, overall structure is reviewed, with commonsense, to bring out the meanings to answer our main research question and conclude as useful knowledge.

5.2.3. Ethical issues during interview

According to our research method, interview, it is individual that conversational nature of interview situations highlights many of the basic ethical issues of any research or evaluation method. Patton had defined five ethical issues that we should concern during the interview period which consist of confidentiality, informed consent, risk assessment, promises and reciprocity, and interviewer mental health (Patton, 1990).

Based on our data collection method, interview had conducted between researcher and companies, confidential data had been asked to show which is big issue in ethic is concerned in this research. Based on Israel's research ethics for social scientists, most guidelines for ethical research require all participants to agree to research before it commences. They typically require that consent should be both informed and voluntary. Informed consent consisted of two activities, first, to create understand in participants, and second is to ask for agree voluntarily to participate the research (Israel & Hay, 2006). During interview, invitation email was sent to the companies, and purpose of the interview has been emailed to the interviewee in advance, permission for confidential data had been asked through email. There are volunteers for companies to participate this research interview without any conditions. Moreover, we were very careful to protect participates from at least physical harm caused by the research interview. Based on the principle of non-malfeasance, contemporary researchers are normally expected to minimize risk of harm or discomfort to participants. In this case, during the interview, interview question must be reviewed, to make sure that any interview question will not cause discomfort or harm to interviewees. For example, some interviewee doesn't want to talk about their product drawbacks, or they don't want to show their experience about CRM implementation project.

5.3. Online survey questionnaires

We have explained about interview methodology in detail, as we mentioned that we are also conducting online survey questionnaires to gather wider empirical data focusing on our research target group (CRM stakeholders) based on our key benefits and drawbacks. Statistical methodology is used to analyze these empirical data and conclusion as value knowledge to support our interview results.

Surveys

Oates stated about surveys that it use idea of sampling to predict pattern of data in larger groups of population (Oates, 2006). In this survey, we prepared a questionnaire for its data generation method. Also, sampling frame is some kind of list or collection of the whole population of people that could be included in survey. In this case, our survey respondents are CRM stakeholders including CRM implementers, CRM providers, and CRM investors. Moreover, our survey is conducted online internet. Oates mentioned that with the use of internet, researchers can conduct survey questionnaire in a very easy and effective way, also less costs and faster time to complete the survey (Oates, 2006). Surveys via questionnaire can be carried out by asking people to visit a website and complete an online questionnaire. Target respondents could be found in company employee email lists, or newsgroup members. But remember that researcher may need to get the permission of the list owner or moderator first. Author also argued that there is no agreement yet on whether internet surveys using questionnaires produce a higher response rate than postal surveys. It is known that unsolicited questionnaires are regarded as junk mail by many people. And it is a good idea to send a short introductory message prior to the actual questionnaire. Another advantage of internet based is, the questionnaire is returned electronically, and the researcher gains the further advantage that the data is already in electronic form, removing the errors creeping in if you type the responses yourself into a software program (Oates, 2006).

Questionnaire

Oates defined about questionnaire that it is pre-defined set of questions with structured form, and then respondent will ask to complete the questionnaire where the result will use to interpret and analyze. Questionnaire can be completed by respondents themselves where researchers don't have to present (Oates, 2006). Question can be designed to generate two types of data: factual data and opinions. Both kinds of data can be collected within one questionnaire, although you need to be clear which kind of data each question is designed to collect. Question can also be divided into open questions and closed questions.

In this research, our survey questionnaire start with gathering information of organization and CRM system of participant, we divide group of participant into 2 groups which are CRM on-premise user/provider and CRM on-demand user/provider. For on-premise participant, we ask them to use their knowledge about CRM on-demand to answer following question about benefits and drawbacks of CRM on-demand compared with their on-premise CRM system, but in case of on-demand participants, we ask them to compare the implementation of CRM on-demand system and on-premise CRM system. Next, coming to main survey questionnaire, based on our research key benefits of SaaS that effect to CRM system, participants will ask to rank the rate for each benefit and drawback by using Likert scale. The Likert scale use for measuring level of agreement on any interest subject or objective criteria where respondents are ask to fill in appropriate level based on their opinion, mostly, five levels of Likert items were used (Likert, 1932).

In this case, five ordered response levels are used in order to measure the attitude of participant in each key factor. The format of Likert scale in our survey is:

- 1 for Strongly disagree
- 2 for Disagree
- 3 for Satisfactory
- 4 for Agree
- 5 for Strongly Agree

Moreover, at the end of each category, survey questionnaire is asked to the participant to rank from the most important (on top) to least important factors (on bottom). All question and answers are in multiply choice with radio-button selection, the reason is to save time and acceptance to participate the survey. Also providing the blank choice on each factor rating question such as "I don't know", in order to create more comfort and trust to the participants for online survey. Our survey questionnaire in detail had shown in appendix C, in topic C.2.

The online survey questionnaire is send through internet to deliver questionnaires to people across the world, with cheap cost and fast time. Questionnaire is held in web form the ability to use web form features such as drop-down menus or radio buttons for the pre-defined responses, it is not yet known whether one is preferable to the other for web questionnaires. Oates said that the electronic form of questionnaire is risky thing, respondents may make mistake, such as using mouse scroll button by accident and rolling the option to unintended answer (Oates, 2006). Through the online survey, we use free website that provide web form survey tool for online survey questionnaire in website www.surveygizmo.com[7]. This website provided all necessary web form tools to create the online survey questionnaire in template, also with pre-statistical analysis for empirical data in their website platforms.

After all, Pilot test will be conducted before launch the questionnaire in order to create content validity in survey questionnaires. Questionnaires are evaluated before used in a pre-test, where its content is shown to people who are experts in either our research domain CRM field. These experts help to refine and improve the questionnaire. Content validity in the questionnaire of our research was approved with the help of our supervisor.

5.4. Data Presentation

After all the data have been collected and the analysis has been completed, the next major task for qualitative researchers is to re-present the study in the form of a paper. The challenge of converting load of data and analysis can be quite great even for the experienced researcher. To help researcher with their efforts at presenting qualitative research in their papers and in their talks, Chenail stated that there are a lot of

---

[7] See detail in Appendix C, C.1

strategies to present the data in good way, each strategy had it own style, it depend on which strategy is suit for their research (Chenail, 1995).

In this case, our research picked the Natural strategies where the data presented in the arrange format. Data is divided into each category which referred to our main research model. Collected and analyzed result is present in each key factors (benefit and drawback of SaaS), further, overall conclusion is presented as main idea to answer the research question in the end.

As we mentioned that we also conducted the online survey questionnaire to collect and analyze statistics which is quantitative data. Statistical methodology will exploit, as Anderson and author's colleagues mentioned that quantitative data are that obtained in interval or ratio scale, which is used to indicate amount of numerical values, such as how much or how many (Anderson et. al, 2007). In our research, tabular and graphical summarizes of data is used as presentation tools for quantitative data in order to present our empirical work and analyzed result in quantitative format. Again as they said that everyone is exposed to these types of presentations, so it is important to understand how they are prepared and how they should be interpreted. It is formal way to present quantitative data in these formats.

5.5. Validating and Reliability

Now turn to the issue of how to get beyond the extremes of a subjective relativism where everything can mean everything. In traditional research terms, this means of determining reliability (how consistent the findings are) and validity (whether the study really investigates what you intended to investigate). In qualitative studies, one important way to verify finding and create validity in research is to ask confirmation about transcripts or analyzed results from interview participants, where they can review their answers and comment on our results (Kvale, 1996).

According to Yin, author stated about construct validity that *"establishing correct operational measures for the concepts being studied"* (Yin, 2003). In order to enhance the construct validity for this research study, data were collected through multiple sources (as we mentioned, interview and survey questionnaire), which using the same logical stream problem to the presentation of data and following same analytical consideration. Moreover, the criteria of reliability concerned with demonstrating the operations of a study, where the data gathering procedures can be repeated with the same results. Also Yin mentioned that reliability aims at minimizing errors and biases in a study (Yin, 2003). In this study, attempts to reduce the biases have been made by carefully describing the problem area and research model in order to create good research question, also carefully describing the data collection method.

To increase the validity and reliability of the research instrument, used to collect data, pilot test is used in order to make sure that our interview guide will be validate and reliability, some suggestion from pilot test resulted in modification of the interview. And also interview guide was sent in advance to participant for review and preparation. Moreover, before launch our online survey questionnaire, questionnaire was reviewed in advance by researchers and our supervisor who is an expert in CRM field and gave suggestions in correcting questionnaires, thus higher level of validity and reliability could be achieved. Suggestion from this group resulted in an additional modification of the interview guide and online survey questionnaire.

Moreover, during the interview, interviewer asked the question controlled by interview guide which hold by interviewer and interviewee. Interview questions designed to ask participant's opinions and facts of CRM on-demand service in their companies, questions will not ask too specific and scoped participants, it will open the gap for participants to talk what they feel like but within the scope specific in interview guide. Also, interviewee were contacted in advance about the matter were going to be discussed and also to assure that they are qualified for our interview.

Furthermore, Oates stated that to conduct quality survey, researchers should concern about validity and reliability (Oates, 2006). First, to create content validity in our survey, literature review is used to verify content in survey questionnaire; expert is asked to verify our questionnaire in pilot test. Next, in construct validity, we had measure the right information we want. And last is reliability the result should be same when same respondents repeat it again.

5.6. Empirical Work

After we had selected research methodology for our research in previous topic, this topic we are going to discuss the planning for evaluation of CRM as a Service's benefits and drawbacks. We will get into specific CRM field in order to study and evaluate empirical data. We have conducted interviews in order to investigate CRM as a Service by interview CRM on-demand vendors who are expert in this area. Also, we had conducted the survey questionnaire for evaluating benefits and drawbacks in wider inspection with respondents' group aim to CRM stakeholders, such as CRM customers and CRM providers.

As we mentioned that our research purpose is to investigate how SaaS improve CRM as a Service compared with tradition CRM on-premise, by doing this, benefits and drawbacks of SaaS that affect to CRM as a Service solution is evaluated. We have evaluated 12 key benefits and 9 drawbacks through face-to-face interview with experts and conducted survey questionnaires to gather more wide view of investigation. Our interview questions is related to key benefits and drawbacks, agreement in each key benefit/drawback from experts were asked based on their experience and opinion in CRM field, including explanation to support their opinions. Moreover, with survey questionnaire, we collected important key factor that is rated from strongly agree to strongly disagree, and also ranked the most important factors to least important factors in each category by respondents based their experience and opinion.

5.6.1. Pilot test

We conducted the pilot test experiment before conducting the actual interview and online survey questionnaire on SaaS's benefits and drawbacks. The purpose of this pilot test was to gather maximum data and information to make sure that our interview questions and survey questionnaire will work in effective and efficient way, and it will not confuses the participant and confirms that we can gather correct information which use in further analysis and conclusion.

Interview question pilot test
Before we conduct our interview, set of interview question have reviewed by CRM expert. Each questions had been commented by CRM expert and the comments were used to re-design the questions set, also questions that can advantage to our research purpose were added. Moreover, our research purpose, research model and interview questions had sent to interviewees in advance as preparation, in order to make sure that interviewees have further understood the interview purpose and they can understand well in interview question.

Survey questionnaire pilot test
The survey questionnaire, pilot test was done in our online survey. Again, the questions in the survey were reviewed by CRM expert to make sure that our questionnaire does not confuse participants. According to the comments questions were corrected. Survey questions have re-designed in order to make comfortable to survey participants. For example, to make sure that some question not necessary to answer, or when participant do not understand question they are able to skip or answer "I don't know" choice. The reason is, our survey is held on internet, we have to make sure that participant have their own right to answer everything, and not to force them in any answers. After we finished correcting all interview questions and survey questionnaire, all set of questions has send to same CRM expert person for the last confirmation for the pilot test.

5.6.2. Empirical study by interview
Interview was conducted with different CRM expert comprised of both open-ended and close-ended questions. At the beginning, introduction question have asked in order to gather information about their CRM system as a background, interviewer will ask participant to explain about their CRM system, what type of CRM system they have, and how can CRM system improve their organization or their customer's organization. The interviewer wanted to inquire the CRM expert about their view on benefit and drawback of SaaS that affect to CRM as a Service solution. Next, coming to the main question, there are two main categories in the interview questions about benefits of SaaS and drawbacks of SaaS. Questions were asked to interviewee about each benefit and drawback of SaaS, in order to evaluate the benefit and drawback of SaaS. Comparing between CRM on-demand and CRM on-premise each factor was explained by interviewer and their agreement was asked to the question, such as Do you agree or yes/no question which consider as close-ended question. Also alternative question have been asked like explanations to support their short answer such as why or how, which consider as open-ended question. Also interview questions are asked in order, step by step, through each factor categories as seen in appendix B, in topic B.1.

5.6.3. Empirical study by online survey questionnaire
In survey questionnaire, our survey is conducted in wider view than interview, participants were selected randomly the CRM stakeholders including both CRM on-premise and CRM on-demand, also with sample of CRM users and providers. The purpose of survey questionnaire is to evaluate the benefits and drawbacks of SaaS that affect to CRM as a Service solution in quantitative result aspect. During the survey sampling, interviewed participants have asked to participate in the survey, and

online survey to send to their customers to participate in our online survey, reference of interview key person was used in order to create trust in our online survey. Moreover, random emails have been sent to CRM stakeholders and ask them to participate in the online survey, participant right was shown at the beginning of the email and online survey, and reference from our supervisor and university was also shown in order to create trust on participant.

Moreover, questions in the questionnaire which force respondents to chose from a range of answers that pre-defined. About format of questions and responses, the "Likert scale" from 1 (strongly disagree) to 5 (strongly agree) is used to collect degree of agreement or disagreement in each key benefits and drawbacks (Likert, 1932). Also apply rank order question to rank the important key factors in each benefits and drawbacks category. After all, all results from questionnaire will collected in form of pre-data and used for analyze in analysis process by using statistical methodology.

5.6.4. Sampling and List of organizations, experts involved

In order to complete our research purpose, information was collected from empirical study. Our target sample is CRM experts who have experience in CRM on-demand service. In order to investigate key benefits and drawbacks that affect to CRM as a Service, our research sample should have good knowledge in CRM on-demand and experience in real world CRM on-demand implementation. Therefore, CRM on-demand providers, who are providing CRM on-demand services is our sampling target, the reason is that in order to evaluate CRM on-demand service, CRM on-demand providers are people who have good understanding on CRM on-demand services and can acknowledge well about it benefits and drawbacks. Moreover, we had selected our participant as contact persons in management level, where those people in management level have well knowledge in CRM on-demand service and have good experience in this field.

Key persons who are expert in CRM field were interviewed, their CRM on-demand services were collected, and this information is used for further analysis process. Interview results of CRM on-demand vendors, companies' information, and their CRM on-demand service are shown here (see interview transcriptions in appendix B, B.2).

CenturioCRM Ltd.
Company 1: CenturioCRM Ltd.
Date of interview: 29 April 2009
Interview Type: Face-to-face
Company Type: CRM on-demand Provider
Address: Reprovagen 12, Taby, Stockholm, Sweden
Website: www.centuriocrm.se
Contact Person: Michael Duffy
Position: CEO/President
Email: Michael.duffy@centuriocrm.se

CenturioCRM is the leading provider of customer relationship management (CRM) software provided on-Demand from a high-security datacenter in Sweden maintained

24/7/365. Nowadays, CenturioCRM has operations in England, Sweden, Denmark, Norway, Finland, Czech Republic and Slovakia. Our interview was performed with Michael Duffy who is CEO and president of CenturioCRM. CenturioCRM have unique strategies to implement CRM on-demand, their strategy is to implement new CRM system from the bottom, as his quote, "CRM is one the application but it is business process". Author is focusing on business process, and re-building the best CRM system that suit to their customers' business processes; moreover, they providing their customers the on-demand service perspective. Also, author mentioned that "It is easy to buy CRM system and is easy to find CRM vendors, but the core problem is that not which vendors you should hire, but it is how you have run the home work (business process), and it is very important to pin point the SaaS aspect".

Connectia Ltd.
Company 2: Connectia Ltd.
Date of interview: 24 April 2009
Interview Type: Face-to-face
Company Type: CRM on-demand Provider, b2bCRM partner
Address: Nørre Farimagsgade 45, DK-1364 København K, Denmark
Website: http://www.connectia.dk/
Contact Person: Nicklas Abrahamsson
Position: CRM on-demand Consultant
Email: nca@connectia.dk

Connectia is CRM vendor providing CRM on-demand service to their customers, Connectia is b2bCRM partner (see b2bCRM detail in appendix A, A.4), they are implementing the CRM of b2bCRM system in Sweden, and their target is to use b2bCRM system to achieve large target group in Sweden. Our contact person is Nicklas Abrahamsson; author is working as consultant in Connectia and also working in implementation team as project manager. Author said that their system is quite easy to do with target group in Sweden and a lot of possible customers asking for their system. They provide two types of CRM on-demand, one is the business-to-business (b2b), CRM system that connects to organization and another one is business-to-customer (b2c) for direct customers.

Logica Ltd.
Company 3: Logica Ltd.
Date of interview: 24 April 2009
Interview Type: Face-to-face
Company Type: CRM on-demand Provider, Microsoft CRM dynamic partner
Address: Ö. Varvsg. 2, 203 13, Malmö, Sweden
Website: http://www.logica.se /
Contact Person: Johan Jöhansson
Position: CRM on-demand project manager
Email: joh.jonsson@logica.com

Logica is IT Consultant Company providing IT solution to their customers. Logica have many branches around the world in Europe, Asia Pacific, America, and Middle East of Africa. But here, we are focusing on their CRM business, and we conducted the interview with Johan Jöhansson, author was working as developer with different kind of CRM system, and now he is working as Project Manager in CRM on-demand which focusing on Microsoft CRM dynamic (see Microsoft CRM dynamic in appendix A, A.3). Logica working as CRM consultant, they don't sale pre-define package but they sale package out of the box, which comes as Microsoft CRM solution package, and they customize it as what customers' need. Also, author said that the benefit of CRM on-demand solution is everything is in one page, also how much money their customer can save, but on top of that, it depended on how much technique they require.

5.7. Summary

The research model is used as an investigation tool for our empirical study. Both qualitative and quantitative methods are used for gathering the information for the research. To collect wide information, both from users and vendors of CRM on-demand system interview method and an online survey questionnaire method is used to collect the empirical data for our analysis. The first two stages of an interview study is Thematizing and Designing. The interview procedure followed by different process mentioned by others authors, in order to conduct good quality research, ethic issues should be concerned as high priority. Based on our data collection method, interview is conducted between researcher and companies; confidential data had been asked to show during the empirical study, big issues of ethic is concerned in this research. Moreover, the interview is recorded by a tape recorder and then translated in to a written form, and then analyze data by using five approaches analysis method. To increase the validity and reliability of the research instrument pilot test is used in order to make sure that our interview guide is validate and reliability, some suggestion from pilot test resulted in modification of the interview guide. Beside, an online survey questionnaire is conducted by preparing a questionnaire and was sent to different companies through the vendors we interviewed and some related companies we knew; survey results were applied statistical method for analysis and interpret parts. After collecting the empirical data next step is to represent the study in the understandable form. At the end of chapter, our empirical work processes were shown, pilot test of interviews and online survey questionnaire were conducted to improve the quality of the processes. Interview questions were asked by following the interview guide, and online survey questionnaire was conducted based on Likert scale to measure agreement of respondents in each benefit and drawback factor, finally, CRM on-demand providers was chose as sampling target group for interview, and interviewed vendors' customer was asked to participate online survey questionnaire, including random emails were sent to related companies in our research field. And, list of persons and organizations that involved in this research also provided.

6. Results and Analysis

After we collected empirical data from the methodology explained in the last chapter, this chapter shows the result of collecting empirical data and result of analyzing collected data through evaluation of benefit and drawback factors. There are two types of a result that are given in this chapter, first is the result from depth interview with CRM experts, and second is result that derived from online survey questionnaire.

6.1. Interview results and analysis

After we had interviewed those experts from different companies with different perspectives here we will analyze data that we gain from interview. First, all conversation is translated into text as we have already mentioned in transcription process. Next, 5 approaches method was applied to analyze the interview data. First approach is condensation; we will condense the information to more brief and valuate in few word. Second approach is categorization; we divided interview information into each category based on our key factors in research model such as Low cost and price in benefit aspect or Security in drawback aspect. Third approach is narrative structuring, in this step, we tried to narrow down the information in each category into more structure, in this case, agree and disagree is used for structuring the information in each category. Fourth, meaning interpretation, we interpret the meaning of the structure by finding the support reason from alternative question that we had asked, and try to understand why they agree or disagree on each category. Last, fifth approach, ad hoc method, after all, we tried to generate meaning from previous approaches result and conclude as final result.

Based on first three stages of analysis, the results of categorize interview results shown in separate tables for each benefit and drawback below. The results are shown in the table had divided into each company opinions with the explanation as the supported reason for their answer, also the structures were lessened into brief and meaningful content. Moreover, in order to interpret the categorized data, next step are interpretation and meaning generation, we interpreted each key factor separately to investigate each key factor that affect to CRM on-demand solution based on results from interview, the results of meaning generation shown separately under each categorized tables.

Categorize and analysis of 12 key SaaS's benefits

Low cost and price

Benefits	Companies	Agree/ Disagree	Explanation
Low cost and price	Connectia	Agree	Depending on lot of factors
	Logica	Depend	It is a bit hard to say yes or no. It depends on customer if they need a lot of integration, so it is not good for them. But they have good system and integration system to serve them, so it is yes.
	CenturioCRM	Agree	-

Most of CRM experts agreed that SaaS can reduce cost and price in CRM implementation. But somehow, it depends on a lot of factors such as integration with legacy system, complicate system. Moreover, some experts said that if they have good configuration and integration platform, it can consider as major benefit of SaaS and it can help to reduce total cost of ownership in CRM implementation.

Low up-front costs and IT initial costs

Low up-front costs and IT initiative costs	Connectia	Agree	One, web based you don't have to put new software in computer, two no maintenance on each PC computer, And three, system is very easy to adapt to Microsoft system
	Logica	Agree	Yes, of course, if you don't have to buy the service. Depend on what kind of system they run. Some companies are not ready for on-demand, but some is already started
	CenturioCRM	Agree	The problem is when compared with the traditional CRM, when you are doing the price calculation in software as a service; you buy the service when everything is included, including the platform infrastructure.

In this benefit, every expert agreed that there is no doubt on this factor that SaaS can reduce low up-front cost and IT initial costs in CRM system. CRM on-demand is web based, there is no need to install new software in client, also don't have to maintain on each PC computer. Further, when compared with the traditional CRM in price calculation in software as a service platform, we can buy the service when everything is included such as the platform infrastructure. Nevertheless, some experts said that it depends on what kind of system they run, some companies may not be ready for CRM on-demand based on complication of their system, but some are already started.

Low implementation and investment risk

Low implementation and investment risk	Connectia	Agree	When implementation fails, it is not because people don't want to use the system. But mostly, they don't see how the system help them to improve the way their work.
	Logica	Disagree	Not have hardware implementation is not the problem.
	CenturioCRM	Agree	-

As interviewed result shown that SaaS is low implementation and low investment risk during the implementation, most of the CRM experts agreed to this benefit, but divergence point is that, with hardware aspect, there is not the problem but integration with other system is the problem that can cause failure in implementation. Moreover, when implementations fail, it's not because of people don't want to use the system, but mostly, they not see how the system helps them to improve the way they work. In summary, every expert agreed that SaaS can get rid of implementation risk, but there are more factors that are related to the failure of CRM implementation, so it is not consider as major benefits.

Clear cost prediction

Clear cost prediction	Connectia	Agree	It is very easy to estimate, because each license to each customers.
	Logica	Agree	But up-front at the beginning is might be less money, but in long term is same.
	CenturioCRM	Agree	The good thing of SaaS is organization that buys it, they know exactly cost at the base, and there are no surprises.

There is quite clear that SaaS can create clear cost prediction over the period, it is easy to estimate because each license assign to each client's user account. And customers know exactly cost at the base, without the hidden cost. But in the long term, some experts didn't see any difference between on-premise and on-demand system. They agree that, at first, up-front can be less money, but in long-term there might be some additional costs occurred such as re-design application based on business process changed.

Not locked into long license

Not locked into long license	Connectia	Agree	Like mobile contract
	Logica	Agree	You can change every time you want
	CenturioCRM	Agree	We are open, we have a long term relationship with our customers, but we not lock up the client

The great benefit of SaaS is that it can get rid of locked into long license problem from provider. With this regard, mostly contract in SaaS is made annually, and customers can cancel it anytime their want. One CRM provider said that we are open and we have a long term relationship with our customers, but we don't locked-up the clients. Also they said that, good example of CRM on-demand contract is the mobile contract, customer have more freedom to decide their usage commitment.

Ease of deployment and management

Ease of deployment and management	Connectia	Disagree	One is not better that other one when it comes to management. I don't see any benefits in this point in SaaS as manager
	Logica	May be	Small and less complex, you will get benefits in on-demand, but if they have existing system, the work is same. On-premise is much longer implementation process, but due to the complicate of the system.
	CenturioCRM	Agree	Everything is included

In ease of deployment and management benefit, there are some doubts on this key benefit. Some CRM experts said that when it comes to management level, they don't see any difference in this point as the manager; also another expert said that, with small and less complex companies, they will get benefits in on-demand, but if they have existing system, the work is same. In fact, on-premise is much longer implementation process but due to the complication of the system. As a result, CRM on-demand can benefit on this point, but it still not strong benefit and it has many factors to end that it is definitely benefit of SaaS.

Fast implementation

Fast implementation	Connectia	Agree	Very fast
	Logica	Agree	Definitely agree
	CenturioCRM	Agree	Agree, could be very different, depend on cost of project

There is no doubt on this benefit; every participant in the interviews has agreed that SaaS can improve the implementation speed of CRM on-demand solution. Compared with traditional on-premise CRM, it could be faster, because there is no need to setup new hardware and IT infrastructure. But it also depends on how complex the system is.

No need IT infrastructure and free up internal resource

No need IT infrastructure and free up internal resource	Connectia	Agree	All is in vendors
	Logica	Agree	You don't need IT to take care server, but still need some IT staff
	CenturioCRM	Agree	When you are selling the software as a service solution, you can go directly to the top and do everything with them, you don't have to talk with the left parts.

Interviewed results show that SaaS platform can free-up internal resource in organization, where vendor will take care for everything. But somehow, it still needs some IT staffs in organization such as IT helpdesk staff. In additional, another advantage of SaaS is, when they are selling the software as a service solution, they can go directly to the top management level and do everything with them, and you don't have to talk with the leave parts, which can have free time and money.

Mobility

Mobility	Connectia	Agree	-
	Logica	Agree	If you can use internet with IE, you can access to the system.
	CenturioCRM	Agree	SaaS is the internet web-based solution; everything is accessed in the mobile, if the mobile have the web browser.

Every expert agreed that, mobility is a major advantage of CRM on-demand solution that users can access to system anywhere with internet through internet browser. One CRM expert said that, SaaS is the internet web-based solution; everything can be accessed in the mobile, if the mobile have the web browser.

High and fast ROI

High and fast ROI	Connectia	Agree	It's fast ROI. Ok, but you not sure about high
	Logica	Not sure	Yes and No, due to the complex of the system and business. It is not different between on-premise and on-demand except h/w and license.
	CenturioCRM	Agree	-

With return of investment part, some CRM experts said that it is fast ROI because of low upfront cost, but author is not sure about high ROI or not. It does not depend on complexity of the system and business process, there is no different between on-premise and on-demand, except hardware and license part.

Flexibility to change usage commitments

Flexibility to change usage commitments	Connectia	Agree	but never have the question from customer about this
	Logica	Disagree	it is same as on-premise system. I mean the way we have to work.
	CenturioCRM	Agree	Agree, you have much flexibility to do the change in SaaS environment compared with the traditional system. Because SaaS solution is build on modern technology which is web-based, so you have more possibility with role management and term management than most system had

Most of CRM expert agrees on this benefit that, SaaS is much flexible to make changes in SaaS environment compared with the traditional system. Because SaaS platform is build on modern technology which is web-based, so they have more possibility with role management and term management than most system had. But in same point, the way to work is same when compared with traditional CRM on-premise system.

Responsibility is on the vendor

Responsibility is on the vendor	Connectia	Agree	-
	Logica	Disagree	Customers should see vendors more often
	CenturioCRM	Disagree	In term of delivery SaaS, it is important that the vendors have the normal knowledge and technical evaluate, how to delivery CRM.

There are some rejection on this benefit, some of CRM experts said that they don't agree with this benefit, because customers should see vendors more often in order to share the knowledge and working process between vendor and customer. Also, one expert said that CRM is not software, CRM is the process, where you need to adopt the process in "how company will work", and then you have customer relationship management. But in other hand, vendor taking care for CRM system is good and their customers can focus on their core businesses. In this benefit, it is a benefit and the responsibility is on the vendor, but the relationship between customer and vendor should not be ignored.

Categorize and analysis of 9 key SaaS's drawbacks

Security

Drawback	Companies	Agree/ Disagree	Explanation
Security	Connectia	Disagree	Because all information belongs to customers, I don't have right to use it. Of course, I might mistake and use it, but they will sue me as against of the contract in security issue
	Logica	Agree	Need to explain the security issue to those customers, and on-premise system also have security problem too.
	CenturioCRM	Disagree	You should reverse the question said what security do you have in your organization. Because our security is equal to the bank and our service need to be available all 24hrs and all year. And our customer have separated and different database system. And data in there is encrypted, we not allow seeing or using those data.

According to this security issue, most CRM experts disagreed, they said that security protection is very secure system and all information is belonged to customers, providers don't have right to use it, also they have contract about security policy between them. But some CRM experts believe that security is major issue in CRM on-demand, good explanation in security issue need to explain to customers, but again, with traditional on-premise, it also have internal security problem too.

Integration

Integration	Connectia	Agree	When it comes to another system, getting more complicated and then we ask customer, we can adapt it but it will cause a lot of money. Our preference is to change into Microsoft platform data, and it will work very well with that
	Logica	Disagree	They try to avoid this problem, but mostly if they need more integration, they will not choose the on-demand.
	CenturioCRM	Disagree	If you have the open source to integrate them, some of SaaS are quite locked in, it mean that it could be quite difficult to exchange data. But if you have a clear and open interface to exchange the data such as web-service, it should be easier to connect and exchange the data in this solution.

Another main issue is integration problem, CRM on-demand have a weak point in integration system which can consider as main drawback of SaaS. All of CRM experts agree that, they try to avoid this problem, and mostly if they need more integration, they will not choose on-demand system. In addition, if there is a clear and open interface to exchange the data such as web-service, it should be easier to connect and exchange the data in this solution, but again, the more integrated system, the more time and money consumption.

Customization and configuration

Customization and configuration	Connectia	Agree	I try to avoid this problem. When it comes to more complicated, it will cause lot of money. Our system is cover 80% of demand in most business process. I think it enough
	Logica	Agree	But normally, SaaS version don't' come in full package, you can do much more on SaaS compared with on-premise.
	CenturioCRM	Disagree	When customers try to implement something, they not do the business with you. That's why, they are lacking. So, at the beginning, we make sure that we have the right designed system in blueprint and then come to the developing process of the system and then so on.

Most of the CRM experts had agreed that they try to avoid this problem, because of limited interface and functionality of ready-to-use application. But nowadays, CRM on-demand had adapted to more flexible platform to solve this weak point, for example, more modules and more customize interface have provided. Moreover, there is one provider who said that they try to get rid of this problem by re-build of CRM application from the beginning to fix their customer requirement without any ready-to-use application.

Control of application and data

Control of application and data	Connectia	Disagree	They own their application and information.
	Logica	Disagree	I think it is same thing as security, it is only on their feeling, they might feel that it not in their control but actually it is.
	CenturioCRM	Disagree	They do the same thing with the traditional one, and they don't have expert who know well about CRM system

In this drawback, every CRM experts disagreed, they said that customers always had controllability in their application and data, it is only on their feeling, and they might feel that it is not in their control ability but actually it does. Moreover, some experts explained that this kind of technology is still young; it needs time for people to get use to this technology. Additionally, they stated that, in few years, all system will be on-demand.

Reliability and connectivity

Reliability and connectivity	Connectia	Disagree	Most of CRM system is held in internet too. I don't see any different.
	Logica	Disagree	Most of the companies have secure internet connection, and CRM business process is not that complicated, when system is down, it will not effect to the main business process.
	CenturioCRM	Disagree	Disagree, most people have internet today, even, if they don't have it in home, they also have in their mobile, so the only thing you need is browser with internet connection. And in the next 3 years, everything will be in cloud computing, you will see everything is on-demand, everything will deliver over the browser.

With reliability and connectivity, this drawback was totally denied by CRM experts, they explained that most people have internet today, even if they don't have it in home, they also have in their mobile, so the only thing their need is web browser with internet connection. And in the next few years, everything will be in cloud computing, you will see everything is on-demand, everything will be delivered over the browser. But it is still the drawback which is not major drawbacks, most companies have secure internet connection, and CRM business process is not that complicated, when system is down, it will not effect to the main business process. Nowadays, most of CRM system now is held on internet, there is no different between these systems.

Vendor lock-in and long term vendor commitment

Vendor lock-in and long term vendor commitment	Connectia	Disagree	The contract is short contract
	Logica	Disagree	There is no difference between both systems. No matter what the process still same such as migration.
	CenturioCRM	Disagree	Customer they see advantages of this
	Connectia	Disagree	When I am talking about CRM system, the information and data is not that much to handle, but comparing with the produce system, it is the hard job to do it
	Logica	Agree	They have a lot of features but compared with on-premise, on-premise is better.
	CenturioCRM	Disagree	We offer from our vendors' perspective, we offer something that advantage for the client.

With this aspect, all CRM experts disagree on this drawback, they didn't see any difference between on-premise and on-demand in this perspective. No matter what the process is, the processes still same such as data migration process. In other hand, customers see this as advantage for flexibility to change contract from vendors, where most of CRM on-demand has a short contract period.

Lack of flexibility, offering, features and functionality

Lack of flexibility, offering, features and functionality	Connectia	Disagree	When I am talking about CRM system, the information and data is not that much to handle, but comparing with the produce system, it is the hard job to do it
	Logica	Agree	They have a lot of features but compared with on-premise, on-premise is better.
	CenturioCRM	Disagree	We offer from our vendors' perspective, we offer something that advantage for the client.

For this drawback's point of view, SaaS created limitation on flexibility, offering, features, and functionality in CRM on-demand, but nowadays, CRM on-demand providers try to get rid of this problem by providing more offer, feature, and functionality in their product. But with on-premise, it still best choice for customers in this point of view.

Low CRM benefits

Low CRM benefits	Connectia	Agree	If I work in back office, then I'm not sure that SaaS can help to improve my work or not.
	Logica	Agree	If you lose some functionality, you also lose CRM benefit. But SaaS is more and more complete, in few year, it will same as on-premise.
	CenturioCRM	Disagree	-

In this drawback, it is related to previous drawback which is lack of flexibility, offering, features and functionality, CRM experts said that if you lose some functionality, you also lose CRM benefit. But somehow, SaaS is more and more complete, in few years, it will same as on-premise. And this drawback of SaaS will be eliminated.

Culture difference

Culture different	Connectia	Disagree	-
	Logica	Agree	I think there are a lot of concerns in this area. SaaS is good for young people and new modern company.
	CenturioCRM	Disagree	I will not say that it cause the problem in work, people that are use to work with the internet, they adopt very quick

Most of experts agreed that CRM on-demand can cause culture difference in the work system in different parts of the world or between the people. They stated that SaaS is good for young people and modern thinking company. But in same way, people that are used to work with the internet, they have capacity to adapt the working style very quick and ready to get the new way of working.

6.2. Survey questionnaire results and analysis

During empirical study, we follow the procedure to design the questionnaire according to the research strategies. We had sent the questionnaires to CRM stakeholders to evaluate benefits and drawbacks of SaaS that affect to CRM as a Service via email, and physical contact. Unfortunately, as a survey questionnaire results, we received only 9 responses from CRM stakeholders, 6 of responses are CRM users and 3 of responses are CRM providers. The respondents have different thoughts regarding to the benefit and drawback of SaaS, but mostly they have the relative comments very significant for the evaluation.

Table 6-1 Summary of survey questionnaire result in key benefits
Note: Level 1 for Strongly Disagree, 2 for Disagree, 3 for Satisfactory, 4 for Agree, 5 for Strongly Agree.

Benefits	Not understand	Level 1	Level 2	Level 3	Level 4	Level 5	Average rate
Agreed							
Mobility	0%	0%	0%	20%	40%	40%	4.2
Low up-front costs and IT initiative costs	0%	0%	0%	20%	60%	20%	4.0
No need IT infrastructure and free up internal resource	0%	0%	0%	20%	60%	20%	4.0
Satisfied							
Low implementation and investment risk	0%	0%	20%	0%	60%	20%	3.8
Ease of deployment and management	0%	0%	0%	40%	60%	0%	3.6
Fast implementation	0%	0%	0%	40%	60%	0%	3.6
Responsibility is on the vendor	0%	0%	40%	20%	40%	0%	3.0
High and fast ROI	0%	0%	40%	20%	40%	0%	3.0
Disagreed							
Low cost and price	20%	0%	0%	40%	40%	0%	2.8
Not locked into long license	20%	0%	0%	40%	40%	0%	2.8
Flexibility to change usage commitments	20%	0%	40%	0%	40%	0%	2.4
Clear cost prediction	40%	0%	0%	20%	40%	0%	2.2

Above table 6-1 shows the percentage of the CRM stakeholder's response against the key benefits that we had chosen for evaluating CRM as a Service. Each key benefit is comprised on one question. We had calculated the percentage of each benefit, also with the average rate based on number of respondent to show level of agreement on each key benefit. Based on the results, it shown most of respondents agreed that mobility, low implementation risk, and free up internal resource are main benefits of SaaS that effecting CRM on-demand solution. But in other hand, with cost reduction, clear cost prediction, not locked into long license, and flexibility to change usage commitments were denied from respondents in SaaS's benefits aspect, where most of respondents satisfied with low implementation risk, ease of deployment, fast implementation, high and fast ROI, and responsibility is on the vendor aspects.

Table 6-2 Summary of survey questionnaire result in key drawbacks
Note: Level 1 for Strongly Disagree, 2 for Disagree, 3 for Satisfactory, 4 for Agree, 5 for Strongly Agree.

Drawbacks	Not understand	Level 1	Level 2	Level 3	Level 4	Level 5	Average rate
Agreed							
Reliability and connectivity	0%	0%	0%	60%	0%	40%	3.8
Security	0%	0%	20%	20%	40%	20%	3.6
Integration	0%	0%	20%	40%	20%	20%	3.4
Customization and configuration	0%	0%	0%	60%	40%	0%	3.4
Lack of flexibility, offering, features and functionality	0%	0%	20%	40%	40%	0%	3.4
Control of application and data	0%	0%	20%	40%	40%	0%	3.2
Satisfied							
Culture different	0%	20%	20%	0%	60%	0%	3.0
Disagreed							
Low CRM benefits	0%	0%	60%	20%	0%	20%	2.8
Vendor lock-in and long term vendor commitment	0%	0%	40%	60%	0%	0%	2.6

Above table 6-2 shows the percentage of the CRM stakeholder's response against the key drawbacks that we had chosen for evaluating CRM as a Service. Each key drawback is comprised on one question. We had calculated the percentage of each drawback, also with the average rate based on number of respondent to the show level of agreement on each key drawback. Based on the results, it shown most of respondents agreed that reliability and connectivity, security, integration, customization and configuration, lack of flexibility, and controllability in application and data are main drawbacks of SaaS that effecting CRM on-demand solution. But in other hand, with cultural different was denied from respondents in SaaS's drawbacks aspect, where most of respondents satisfied with low CRM benefits, and vendor lock-in problem.

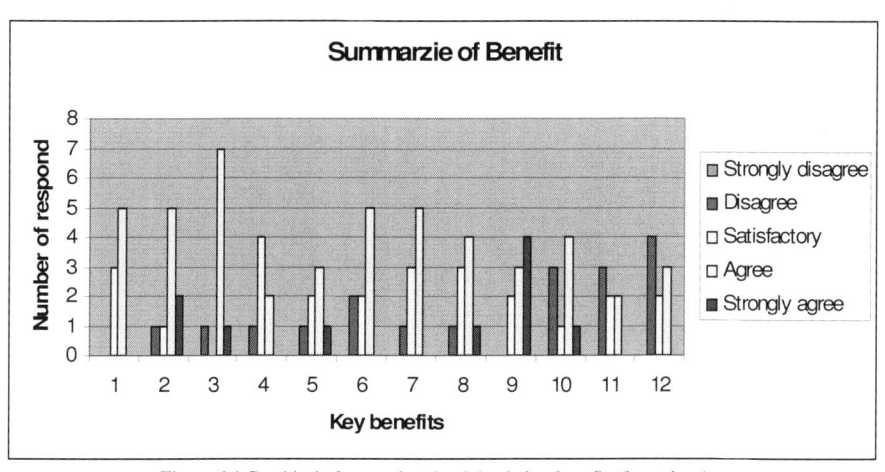

Figure 6-1 Graphical of respondents' opinion in key benefits (by authors)
Note: 1 is Low cost and price, 2 is Low up-front costs and IT initiative costs, 3 is Low implementation and investment risk, 4 is Clear cost prediction, 5 is Not locked into long license, 6 is Ease of

deployment and management, 7 is Fast implementation, 8 is No need IT infrastructure and free up internal resource, 9 is Mobility, 10 is High and fast ROI, 11 is Flexibility to change usage commitments, 12 is Responsibility is on the vendor.

This chart in figure 6-1 depicts the weight age in graphical format where the given numeric values form 1 to 12 shows the each key benefit and each color of graph describe the scale of the agreement of the respondents against the survey questionnaire.

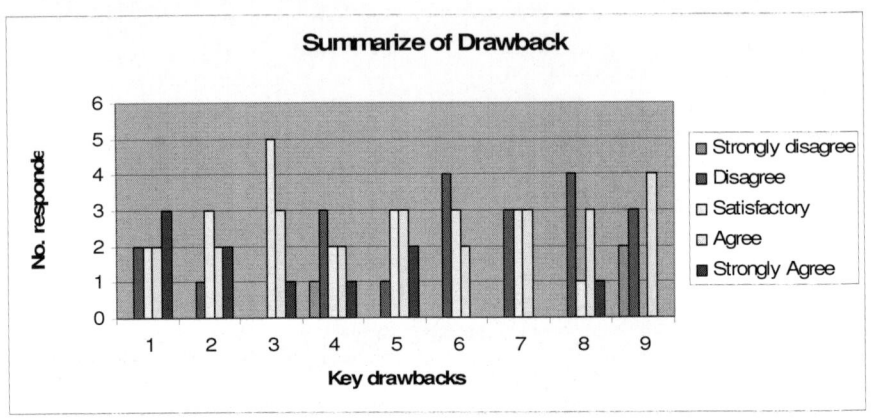

Summarize of Drawback

Figure 6-2 Graphical of respondents' opinion in key drawbacks (by authors)
Note: 1 is Security, 2 is Integration, 3 is Customization and configuration, 4 is Control of application and data, 5 is Reliability and connectivity, 6 is Vendor lock-in and long term vendor commitment, 7 is Lack of flexibility, offering, features and functionality, 8 is Low CRM benefits, 9 is Culture different.

Also this chart in figure 6-2 depicts the weight age in graphical format where the given numeric values form 1 to 9 shows the each key drawback and each color of graph describe the scale of the agreement of the respondents against the survey questionnaire.

Table 6-3 Summary of ranking in key benefits

Value	Average Rank
High level rank	
Low cost and price (Total cost of ownership)	2.2
Low up-front costs and IT initiative costs	2.4
Low implementation and investment risk	3
Middle level rank	
Clear cost prediction	5.1
Fast implementation	5.7
Not locked into long license	6.7
Ease of deployment and management	7
Low level rank	
Mobility	8
No need IT infrastructure and free up internal resource	8.1
High and fast ROI	8.1
Flexibility to change usage commitments	10.8
Responsibility is on the vendor	10.9

Next, each key benefit had been ranked by respondents, results shown in table 6-3, 9 respondents were asked to rank key benefits from most important (1) to least important (12). Above table show average rank of each benefit, as resulted, we have divided key benefits into 3 main groups, first group of high rank, low cost and price, low up-front cost and low implementation risk were voted as high important key factors. Second group is middle level rank, where clear cost prediction, fast implementation, not locked into long license, and ease of deployment are classified in this level. And last group is low level rank which is mobility, no need IT infrastructure, high/fast ROI, flexibility to change, and responsibility on vendor are voted as less important key benefits.

Table 6-4 Summary of ranking in key drawbacks

Value	Average Rank
High level rank	
Integration	2.7
Customization and configuration	2.7
Security	3.2
Middle level rank	
Control of application and data	3.8
Reliability and connectivity	4.2
Low level rank	
Lack of flexibility, offering, features and functionality	6.2
Vendor lock-in and long term vendor commitment	6.7
Low CRM benefits	7.7
Culture different	7.9

Also with drawback, table 6-4 shown the result of drawbacks that ranked by respondents. Each key drawback also had been ranked by respondents, 9 respondents were asked to rank the key drawbacks from most important (1) to least important (9). Above table show average rank of each benefit, as resulted, we had divided result into 3 main groups; first group is high level rank, where integration, customization and configuration, and security are voted as most important weakness of SaaS. Second group is middle level rank, where controllability of application and data, reliability and connectivity are nominated in this group. Last group is low level rank, where lack of flexibility, vendor lock-in, low CRM benefits, and cultural different are chosen as less important weakness of SaaS that affect to CRM on-demand solution.

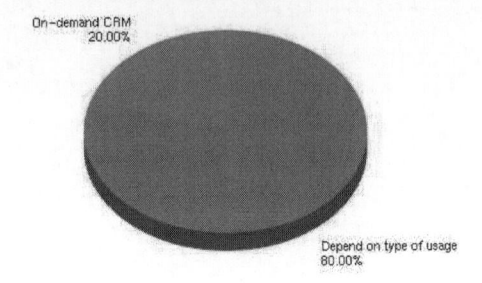

Figure 6-3 Graphical of respondents' opinion in comparison of CRM on-demand and CRM on-premise (by authors)

According to last question in survey questionnaire, we had asked respondents opinion to compare between on-demand and on-premise solution which one is the best choice for them. Above chart shown that, 20% chose CRM on-demand, but 80% said that it's depending on type of usage, with the reason that every companies are different and have different business processes procedure.

6.3. Summary

After the interview and online survey questionnaire processes, all the collected data is analyzed by using the five approaches and statistical method. All the interview data is translated in to text format. We interpreted each key factor separately that affect to CRM on-demand solution based on results from interview by evaluating them into benefit and drawback categories. Also, with the online survey questionnaire method, all the results are analysis and summarized in tabular and graphical format for better interpretation. And all analyzed result will use for discussion and conclusion in next chapter.

7. Discussion and Conclusion

7.1. Discussion

In gathering the empirical data and after analyzing the results taken from the investigation the various issues and difficulties of each key benefit and drawback become clearer. To sum up, this research conducted for investigate key benefit and drawback that affect to CRM as a Service system, by using in-depth interview with CRM experts as main empirical study method, also with survey questionnaire helped to verify our conclusion. In this chapter, we will discuss the results, finding from evaluation methods. The first part of this chapter depicts the discussion on key benefits and drawbacks. Then next, we have concluded overall result of the main result to answer our research question. At last, implication of research and future work has explained.

7.1.1. Investigation of Software as a Service in CRM

In our investigation, we have evaluated each key benefit where discussion after interviewing shown that it depend on many factors, yet the most important factor towards the customer in CRM implementation is low cost when compared it with on-premise system. According to questionnaire, the level of agreement in term of cost reduction when applying CRM, it has shown that average rate is 2.8 which is not consider as highly agreed, and shown that most of audiences consider about post-phrase in maintenance. Moreover, the other core benefit of implementing to CRM on-demand has the level of agreement as 4.0, which means that there is no need to buy infrastructure then the SaaS can reduce the low up-front cost and IT initials.

In addition, low risky in CRM implementation has found in audience aspect with level of agreement at 3.8. Its implementation of CRM on-demand is fast because no need to set up the new hardware and server, it is ready to utilized software system with all features like "instant food" when compared to the on- premise system. Moreover, SaaS works like a mobile service with access of internet, therefore, this service steadily provides for the users to access to the system from any place, which has the level of agreement as 4.2 in Mobility benefit factor.

One or other way it is simple for the customer to cancel the license because the license is not long run agreement. Due to CRM on-demand, the vendors do not lockup the customers with long run contract. That is why time period might convince the customers to break the contract if they want to do so. And the customers have the freewill to decide their usage commitment; one expert said that it is same as usual cell phone contract, and it also provided ability to estimate their cost evidently. In addition, SaaS platform is web based technology, it can provide flexibility to do the change in SaaS environment better than traditional system.

Yet, somehow, not every benefit of SaaS will be affected to CRM system effectively, we had found that there are some benefits of SaaS which are not major benefits, no difference between on-demand and on-premise system such as in ease of deployment and management, when it comes across management phrase, there is no difference between both systems, even the work processes are the same. Moreover, the return of investment aspect, on-demand benefit on hardware and license part, but more or less equally cost. Basically, it is not the major benefit of SaaS, eventually, sometime when everything it is responsibility of vendors, it can cause the problems hence; most of the providers suggest customers should see vendors more often in order to share the knowledge and working process between vendor and customer.

In drawback part, from previous research; security is critical problem in CRM system. But in our discussions and after interviewing security is not considered to be an immense drawback because with one of interviewee, one vendor, when we discussed about this issue he mentioned that:

Interviewer: Security is a drawback do you agree with that? Please explain.
Interviewee: No not at all what kind of security do you have in your system?

Surprisingly, he meant what kind of security the customers have in their system? Even he does not believe that security is drawback. Still after discussions with other interviewees, we found that security is not a critical drawback, as the result of questionnaire shown 3.6 level of agreement.

Yet, in our early discussion mentioned, one of the key drawbacks is integration problem, which is considered as a main drawback of SaaS. Unexpectedly, the vendors try to avoid this problem, and even attempt to evade the problem of customization and configuration due to limitation of interface in ready to use application, where level of agreement of integration and customization is same at 3.4 which consider make both of these drawbacks as main drawback of SaaS. One of key drawbacks is being negligible by the vendors is reliability and connectivity of the CRM on-demand solution, with support by level of agreement in 3.8, as this system is works with a web browser and internet connection only. And may be in next few years everything will be in clouds, eventually, everything will be delivered with browser, problematically, most of the work could be done on internet, yet in many parts of the world, the internet connection is still not reliable and flexible.

Moreover, applying this application in the organization, the users should be well trained in order to use the system otherwise it may effect on usage of the system in a negative way and may get terrible critics. In other hand, some key drawbacks were eliminated by time; advance technology was solving these weaknesses point of SaaS. In controllability of application and data, everybody disagreed to this point, it's because only the feeling of customers, also vendors locked-in and long term commitment, the work process is same as on-premise system, and there is no difference between both system when it come to phrase of maintenance. Moreover, with the lack of flexibility of offering in SaaS platform, definitely, it is one of the weakness in CRM on-demand, but nowadays, CRM on-demand is more and more completely, and this problem will eliminate by time, as well with the low CRM benefits problem, because of low offering in CRM functionality, will move out too.

7.1.2. Evaluation and validation

It is certainly an aspect of evaluating the quality of a study, and standards vary within the qualitative community. Lincoln (1995) identified eight standards for evaluate the qualitative research in author's book (Lincoln, 1995). Based on Lincoln standards, it will use as guideline for research evaluation, in order to create quality in research, above standards should be reached by researcher. Before interview, interview purpose and prepared questions will be evaluated based on above standards, guidelines for publication should be provided in text and it should have clear and understandable in detail. Moreover, purpose of research should identify at beginning of interview. During the interview period, interviewees will have a chance to express their opinion, but interviewer should have strong understanding about interview purpose and try to control the interview scope in their subject, in this case, researcher should have good understanding in each benefit and drawback, in order to handle and manage the interview period to benefit their interesting subject in high-quality. Furthermore, researcher should understand the difference between real implementation aspect and theories aspect, in real world implementation, our key benefit/drawback factors might not cover all the actual cost during implementing period, the ability in fast understanding and fast adaption is required during the interview. At last, credit about interviewees must give in the research report. For example, companies name should be provided as reference in research report to share their rewards with persons; nevertheless, we asked for their willingness to the public their name or companies name, in order to respect the participant right.

Regarding Validation, the data validation in mixed methodological research is based on the type of research strategy that we had mentioned in our research methodology. Our research consisted of qualitative data (from interview) and quantitative data (from survey questionnaire) in order to investigate benefits and drawbacks of CRM on-demand solution. We had adopted the criteria for validity proposed by the Guba and Lincoln[8].

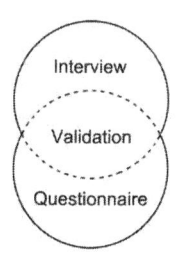

Figure 7-1 Adopted procedure for validation (by Guba and Lincoln)

To validate the results, analyzed result from survey questionnaire had used to verify result from interview method in order to validate empirical study results. Besides, the four criteria for the judgments used for validation in this research are Credibility, Transferability, Dependability and Conformability.

- **Conformability:** refers to the degree to which the results could be confirmed or corroborated by others. In this case, our interview transcription had been sent to interviewees, in order to ask confirmation and correction from them. Moreover, the transcriptions were done twice by different researcher to make sure that we get exactly what we had interviewed.

---

[8] See "Qualitative Validity, from Research Methods Knowledge Base" in reference.

- **Dependability:** means the changing in time and setting affects to results. During the interview, we had controlled the sampling of interviewee in the same business area; all of the participants had been working on CRM on-demand field as their core business. Also, interviews were conducted in the same period of time, in order to make sure that we had been interviewing the right persons in the right period. Based on our research objective, is to investigate CRM as a Service system which is new technology and it always change very fast.
- **Creditability:** mean to describe or understand the phenomena of interest from the participant's eyes, the participants are the only ones who can legitimately judge the credibility of the results. So with this regard, the result had sent back to participants for evaluation and correction, also we gave the interview conversation of 3 interviewees in the appendix B, B.2.
- **Transferability:** mean that result of qualitative research should be able to transfer to other area of contexts. As we mentioned that SaaS platform also applied to other system such as HR system. This result was generated based on benefits and drawbacks of SaaS which is open to transfer and adapt to other system evaluation, but in this case, one threat is to avoid the unique of each system. But somehow, we had selected CRM system because CRM system is the most fashionable in on-demand technology.

Moreover, Denscombe suggested that the analysis of quantitative data should include efforts to ensure that correctly recorded data, measured the right subject, and accurate in analyzed data (Denscombe, 2007). To address these three points, we try to validate our result as follow:

- Using Pilot test to make sure that research instrument does not vary in the results it produces on different occasions when it is used.
- Test the instrument to make sure that respondent provide the same kind of answers to similar question and generally answer in a consistent fashion.
- As we mentioned in transferability, the finding will apply to other people and other contexts.
- Make sure that the analysis is correct, in this case, Software analysis tool can help to reduce the human-error, and make sure that the statistical analyzed data is correct.

7.1.3. Challenges and limitations

Although software-as-a-service for CRM has gained force in SMB, CRM as Service suites for large enterprises remain unclear and that development won't come until 2012 (Gather, 2008). Our conclusion should concern about Small and Medium size of business, not including big size of company. Besides, as we know that SaaS is new technology that still on process to investigates in this technology, few articles were discussed about SaaS and its benefits/drawback. Rare information about this technology is our challenge, to study on SaaS; previous theory will be adapted and applied in our research model. For example, some of benefit/drawback factors that we mentioned might not be completed; some of specific factors in SaaS platform are needed in order to complete the research model. Nevertheless, this research is just beginning of SaaS platform study. Further research may be conducted to improve our research model and construct more knowledge on top of our research model. Another challenge is time, our participants are businessman, and they have no time for our research investigation. It is very hard to get into their work place. Also, the bias aspect, some of participants are CRM providers which always make sure that their product is good, but in other hand, CRM users might not thing like that. During the analysis part, we had to be careful about bias aspect in participant to generate quality in our research conclusion.

Moreover, limited time and money, we have few limitations to our investigation process, such as more interviews should conduct in order to gather vary of resource. Also, with the questionnaire, more respondents should participate our survey questionnaire in order to gain enough sampling to valid the result and conclusion.

7.2. Conclusions
Based on all procedure that we had mentioned above, the purpose of this research is to investigate how SaaS platform affects to CRM as a Service, research methodologies were conducted in order to gather empirical data and analyzing it. In this chapter, methodology that used in this research will be concluded. Also, key issues of the key benefits and drawbacks are concluded. In overall, research is concluding as valuable knowledge and research question will be answered.

7.2.1. Methodology conclusion
To investigate the benefits and drawbacks of SaaS that effect to CRM as a Service solution, the methodology was conducted to reach the research objective. Beginning with literature review, to review all key benefits and drawbacks of SaaS that effect to CRM on-demand solution, related articles were reviewed and evaluated in order to create research model. Next, after we had created research model, interview and survey questionnaire were designed as methodology to gather empirical data. Interview method was conducted as main method to investigate key benefits and drawbacks of SaaS. Also survey questionnaire was conducted as additional empirical data resource in wider inspection to verify the main conclusion. During the analysis process, 5 approaches were applied to analysis procedure for the interviewed data which resulted in qualitative data. Also with survey questionnaire, statistical analysis procedure was applied to analyze quantitative data as result of survey. By doing this, two sources of data were analyzed in different procedures, and they were combining together as the main conclusion.

During the interview with the vendor's aspect we found some bias. Some of them did not accept the drawbacks, they denied but after we have evaluated the benefits and drawbacks, we think that they do not want to accept the drawbacks but in the background they might be trying to overcome these drawbacks.

7.2.2. Research Conclusion
The purpose of this research work was to investigate how Software as a Service (SaaS) platform affects CRM system in CRM as a Service, by doing this, benefits and drawbacks of SaaS, which is collected from literature review and assumed to affect

CRM on-demand solution, were evaluated. To explore each key benefits and drawbacks of SaaS, we have selected the interview as main investigation method. The investigation conducted with CRM experts from empirical world, each key benefits and drawbacks were explained briefly to participants and their agreement to the question were asked based on yes or no answer, including the explanation for their answer. Finally the result taken from benefits and drawbacks evaluation were analyzed and concluded to evaluate the CRM as a Service system. The results were validated for CRM as a Service with conducted online survey questionnaire with CRM stakeholders.

From answers to the research questions, we concluded that SaaS have great benefits in CRM system, it create improvement in CRM implementation, such as low cost, low initial costs, improvement in license term, implementation speed, free up internet resource, and mobility. CRM on-demand is a great innovation applied by SaaS platform to benefit the CRM system. During the research, we had found that great benefits that had strong effect to CRM system are low up-front cost and IT initial cost, low risky in implementation, fast implementation, and usage mobility. But unfortunately, in term of cost reduction and return of investment aspects, its not consider as main benefit of SaaS with the reason that, there is no different between on-demand and on-premise system during post-phrase implementation in maintenance period. Also, based on everything is responded by providers, the results shown that it consider as disadvantage rather than benefit by the fact that customers and vendors should often corporate in order to create efficiency in work process.

In other hand, SaaS also have weaknesses in CRM on-demand such as be fond of integration problem, customization and configuration, reliability and connectivity, lack of functionality, and culture different. According to these disadvantages, it creates doubt on CRM investors who plan to implement CRM on-demand solution. Based on research results, we had found that SaaS can cause the problem to CRM system in integration aspect, customization and configuration aspect, and reliability and connectivity aspect, which consider as major drawbacks of SaaS that affect to implementation of CRM system. However, according the security aspect, the results shown that security is not consider as main problem in CRM as a Service implementation, where it can handled by providers and internal security policy in organization. Also, with advantage of developed advance technologies such as Ajax or XML, it can get rid of lack of flexibility problem in SaaS platform; which used to consider as major drawback in last decade, by providing more and more complete functionality and features in CRM as a Service solution.

To make it more effective for CRM on-demand, mentioned drawbacks should be eliminated, CRM on-demand are need to be improved such as good integration interface, more feature and functionality, ability to customize and configure system. Moreover, we had found that the problem is not only in technology, there are some problems about trust in the on-demand platform based on lack of good understanding and knowledge in CRM on-demand. Besides, CRM on-demand is not suitable for every type of business process, small and less complex company is good for CRM on-demand, but if they have complex business process and big system, investors should have good consideration between CRM on-demand and CRM on-premise which is suitable for their business type.

Nevertheless, as we mentioned that, nowadays CRM on-demand is more and more complete, but somehow SaaS platform is still early stages, more investigation and proofs are needed, time are important factor to prove this technology. Also, in next few years, most of services will delivery as on-demand; this is a good chance to situate more study on SaaS platform in order to prove that this technology is not the mistake.

From this research we have learned that this system have benefits and drawbacks. It's important that the organizations should try to overcome from the drawbacks and should show the strong use of the their system to the user and we think that even the users should try to make their systems better and train the system users so that they do not complain about the system and pose it as a drawback which may affect on the system usage. All through this research we tried to evaluate the benefits and drawbacks now we have gain good understanding about this system.

Last but not least, as we mentioned in theoretical framework that movment of CRM system to cloud computing platform is to improve the business model with subscription model in offering layer, in order to survive in high competition market, where main focus is reducing cost rather than increasing revenue. Related to our research, it may help the audience to make a right decision, to approach or to implement CRM as a Service and can get a good understand about it. Moreover, it can also provide good information about CRM as a Service to the providers and can know what kind of problems does the users is facing and providers can try to overcome these drawbacks.

7.3. Suggestion for further R&D

The question in this research report is to be explored how SaaS platform can affect to CRM as a Service by evaluating key benefits and drawbacks of SaaS. To investigate this, we had selected interview and survey questionnaires method with CRM experts to gather the empirical data in CRM field. The analysis of the result showed that SaaS can benefit the CRM system and improve efficiency of CRM implementation system. But there are still some issues for creating improvement in the CRM as a Service concerning the CRM stakeholders, and we would like to indicate the recommendation on CRM as a Service.

As we know that CRM as a Service or CRM on-demand consider as unstable technology, there are some doubt on these technology, and people are not sure about it. We suggest that more investigation and evaluation on this technology is needed and publish to public in order to create well understanding and clear explanation about this technology in CRM stakeholders, such as key success factors in CRM on-demand implementation. Moreover, most of the vendors trying to get rid of weak points of CRM on-demand, such as security, integration, etc. But somehow, they put too much focus on technology and ignoring their customers' business process. In order to balance these concerns, CRM on-demand solution should develop with the concern of customers' business processes, with the reason that CRM is not the system, but it is the business process. And last, more concern towards globalization should raise, not every country in the world are ready to this web-based platform, there are some countries that not ready for this technology and implementer should concern this issue. For example, CRM on-demand is web-based system which can access through internet, but not every company, in some area, can run their business on internet.

7.4. Future work

As we had mentioned that SaaS platform is quite new technology and it still need more verification, as well, evaluation and investigation are needed in order to improve the SaaS platform and create more trust in this technology to IT investors. Furthermore, to create trusts in CRM as a Service, there are needed to uncover and solve the key successes of CRM as a Service implementation. Next step is how to succeed in implementing CRM as a Service; key successes will define and investigate in order to create costly and trustable services in CRM on-demand system which can benefit to the organization. For example, in order for SaaS to succeed, vendors will have to think more carefully about integration aspect and user management across SaaS.

Appendix A: CRM on-demand providers

A.1: Saleforce.com

Salesforce.com is a vendor of Customer Relationship Management (CRM) solutions; it delivers to businesses over the internet using the software as a service model. Salesforce.com's CRM solution is broken down into several applications: Sales, Service & Support, Partner Relationship Management, Marketing, Content, Ideas and Analytics. Salesforce.com's Platform-as-a-Service product is known as the Force.com Platform. The platform allows external developers to create add-on applications that integrate into the main Salesforce application and are hosted on salesforce.com's infrastructure.

Salesforce.com was founded in 1999 by former Oracle executive Marc Benioff, who pioneered the concept of delivering enterprise applications via a simple web site. Salesforce.com is constantly building on that legacy by improving and expanding their award-winning suite of on-demand applications, their Force.com platform for extending Salesforce, and our one-of-a-kind App-Exchange directory of on-demand applications. Salesforce.com is headquartered in San Francisco, California, with regional headquarters in Dublin (covering Europe, Middle East, and Africa), Singapore (covering Asia Pacific less Japan), and Tokyo (covering Japan). Other major offices are in Toronto, New York, London, Sydney, and San Mateo, California. Salesforce.com has its services translated into 16 different languages and currently has 55,400 customers and over 1,500,000 subscribers. In 2008, Salesforce.com ranked 43rd on the list of largest software companies in the world. (*History and Company definition of Saleforce.com cited from: http://en.wikipedia.org/wiki/Salesforce.com*) for more information please visit website below.

Website: http://www.salesforce.com

A.2: Siebel Systems (Oracle)

Siebel Systems, Inc. was a software company principally engaged in the design, development, marketing, and support of customer relationship management (CRM) applications. The company was founded by Thomas Siebel in 1993. At first known mainly for its sales force automation products, the company expanded into the broader CRM market. By the late 1990s, Siebel Systems was the dominant CRM vendor, peaking at 45% market share in 2002.

On September 12, 2005, Oracle Corporation announced it had agreed to buy Siebel Systems for $5.8 billion. Siebel is now a brand name owned by Oracle Corporation. Siebel Systems, Inc. began in sales force automation software, then expanded into marketing and customer service applications, including CRM. From the time it was founded in 1993, the company grew quickly. Benefiting from the explosive growth of the CRM market in the late 1990s, Siebel Systems was named the fastest growing company in the United States in 1999 by Fortune magazine. With the growth of electronic commerce, Siebel formed strategic alliances and made several acquisitions to provide e-business solutions for CRM and related areas. One secret to Siebel's success was its ability to form alliances; as of late 2000 the company had more than 700 alliance partners. (*History and Company definition of Saleforce.com cited from: http://en.wikipedia.org/wiki/Siebel_Systems*) for more information please visit website below.

Website: http://www.oracle.com/siebel/index.html

A.3: Microsoft Dynamic CRM

Microsoft Dynamics CRM is a Customer Relationship Management software package developed by Microsoft. It is a part of the Microsoft Dynamics family of business tools. Microsoft Dynamics CRM offers flexible software licenses. Microsoft Dynamics CRM offers two types of licenses: Server license and Client Access License (CAL). Each deployment should have at least one server license and one CAL. CAL is also called as user license. There are two types of CAL: First, named user CAL, this is tied with the user name i.e. the user can access MSCRM from any computer. Second, device CAL, this is tied with the Device i.e. CRM can be accessed from only one device. This model is useful in case of Call Center. Dynamics CRM version 4.0 adds a number of new features, including support for duplicate data detection and other enhancements. Perhaps most importantly, CRM 4.0 provides true multi-tenancy, which will allow the creation of multiple organizations on a single server. CRM 4.0 was released with the following improvements:

- More powerful and easier to configure Reporting and BI (now based on SRS instead of Crystal)
- More powerful data import tools, de-duplication capability now included
- Enhanced entity relationships – many to many, self-referential
- Improved programmability - enhanced Web Services, unified event model, plug-ins to replace callouts
- Light enquiry user license now available - potentially reducing the costs associated with rolling out across larger organizations
- Multi Tenancy - One server can host more than one business organization
- Multi Currency
- Multi Lingual
- Microsoft Office Communicator / Windows Live Messenger presence integration support
- Cloud Computing with Microsoft Online Services

(*History and Company definition of Saleforce.com cited from: http://en.wikipedia.org/wiki/Microsoft_Dynamics_CRM*) for more information please visit website below.

Website: http://www.microsoft.com/dynamics/crm/default.mspx

A.4: B2bCRM

B2bCRM is CRM on-demand providers, they offers web-based CRM systems that are easy to start-up and easy to use. Data fields, overviews and reports are easily customized - with no need for consultants. More than 350 companies use b2bCRM every day. It is their policy to continuously enhance the system based on user input - and at the same time maintain simplicity and ease of use. Upgrades take place twice a year, and are done without any user involvement. This is another benefit from the system being web based.

(History and Company definition of Saleforce.com cited from: http://www.b2bcrm.net/about.asp) for more information please visit website below.

Website: http://www.b2bcrm.net/

Appendix B: Interviews

B.1: Interview questions

Introduce questions
- What kind of CRM system do you have/provide in your organization?
- How can CRM system help your organization/customers? And what is it functionality?
- Is your CRM system sufficient for your purposes? Do you have a plan to change your CRM system?

Main questions in Benefits
- Did SaaS reduce cost and price (Total cost of ownership) of the CRM system? And how?
- How can SaaS reduce up-front costs and IT initiative costs? Any effect to implementation process?
- SaaS claim that it has low implementation and investment risk, do you agree with this? Why, why not?
- SaaS can help in the prediction of costs for the organization. Do you agree with this? If so, how?
- SaaS can get rid of being locked in to a long license from a vendor compared with traditional CRM system. Do you agree? Can you give details about this?
- About ease of deployment and management, did SaaS play important rule to improve deployment and management in CRM system compared with traditional CRM system? If so, explain.
- Did SaaS improve implementation speed in CRM on-demand system compared with traditional CRM system?
- During the implementation period, SaaS allow an organization to have no need of an own IT infrastructure and can free up internal resource, do you agree with this? If so, explain
- Did SaaS improve mobility aspects of the CRM on-demand system? Please explain.
- Did SaaS create high and fast return of investment in CRM on-demand system compared with traditional on-premise system?
- Did SaaS allow client to be more flexible to change usage of the CRM as business conditions change? If so, Why?
- Based on SaaS definition, responsibility is on the vendor, do you think it can benefit CRM on-demand customers? Please explain.

Main questions in drawbacks
- Is Security an issue in CRM on-demand? How? Do you have methods to handle this problem?
- Did Integration issues effect to the choice of choosing CRM on-demand system? How can it effect to the system?
- Most of customers concern about customization and configuration problem in CRM on-demand. Do you agree with this proposition? And how it effect to the system?

- In control of application and data, customer will lose the controllability of application and data, do you think these problems will effect to CRM on-demand customer or not? And how can you handle these problems?
- According to SaaS definition, Most of customers have doubt on its reliability and connectivity through the internet browser. Do you think this is a problem? And how can you handle these problems?
- Customers wondering about vendor lock-in and long term vendor commitment. Do you think this is a big disadvantage of SaaS? Do you think it will effect the choice of customers? If yes, how can you explain to customer to tackle these problems?
- Do you think the problem of lack of flexibility, offering, features and functionality are SaaS weakness? If yes, how can you handle these problems?
- According to CRM on-demand definition, SaaS may actually impede the ability to realize full entitlement to CRM value, and it can cause low CRM benefits. Do you agree with this statement? Please explain.
- Do you think that CRM on-demand application will face the culture different problem? Please explain.

B.2: Interview transcriptions
Connectia Ltd.
Interviewer1: Thanawin Ratametha (**I1**)
Interviewer2: Manasa Veeragandham (**I2**)
Interviewee: Nicklas Abrahamsson (**E**)

I1: Our research is talking about CRM as a Service, and we are focusing on its benefits and drawbacks of SaaS that effect to CRM system. So, we would like to investigate about how software as a Service effect to CRM system. Because CRM as a Service is CRM system that applies the SaaS platform to benefits the system in some way. We try to evaluate the benefit of SaaS like reducing cost of ownership, and also with drawbacks too. And we try to compare the new CRM with the old one. We got key benefits and drawbacks from previous research articles and journals in last few years. Our question will relate to these key benefits and drawbacks based on research model.

E: Can u give me few minute to review these key benefits and drawbacks?
I1, I2: Yes, sure
I1: I will begin ask you the question one by one. Ok. First, can u explain your job position?
E: divided into 2 areas, one, I'm responsible person of implementation in CRM of b2bCRM system in Sweden. Second area is I'm working in consultant as well. I try to use b2b CRM system to achieve large of target group in Sweden. The system is quite easy to find the way to due with target group in Sweden and a lot of possible customers asking for this system.
I2: It's mean you are the vendors providing CRM system of b2bCRM.
E: Absolutely
I2: You're partner of b2bCRM

I1: What kind of CRM system does you provided? Just only CRM on-demand?

E: Exactly

I1: How can it help your organization? Do you have a lot of module?
E: It is mainly two ways to help organization. One is the tradition b2b sale, CRM system connects to organization. Another one is b2c to customers.

I1: So, I will begin with the benefit first. Did SaaS reduce cost and price of CRM system? Do you think so?
E: of course.
I1: Can you explain me briefly.
E: It's a lot of reason in this factor.

I1: How can SaaS reduce upfront cost and IT initial cost. It's mean like, you don't have to build everything again and you don't need much time to create everything new again. Do you agree with that? Any effect to implementation process?
E: Yeah, one, web based you don't have to put new software in computer.
I1: Just internet browser?
E: yes, right. Two, you don't have to do the maintenance in each computer such as upgrading computer. And three, system is very easy to adapt to Microsoft system. I mean it is easy compatible to Microsoft system such as outlook, excel, word.
I1: Training program, you mean?
E: Yes, most of the time when you face with CRM system implementation is most of users feel like it is complicate to use the interface of the system. And when you use the same web-based, it use same environment to the Microsoft system, and users will feel more comfortable to use it. Huge benefits, it saves a lot of money.

I1: And about low implementation and investment. Do you agree with that?
E: Yeah, why not.
I1: Can u explain me? How can it get rid of the fail problem in implementation?
E: When implementation fail, it not because people don't want to use the system. But mostly, they not see how the system help them to improve the way their work. Each one, have their own unique ways to work, if I can adapt the system to help them here, make it smooth, then its success. But within this success, if they ask me something, can you system do these, I will go up and ask my back up, they done it in few and then its success. But never make it complicated. And one more thing, if more traditional CRM system, when you want to implement new thing, you have to ask your IT team and it take time (not main focus) and complicate to do it.

I2: So, compared with the new one, its take long times the done the process.
E: yes, it is.

I1: SaaS as you know, it can help in cost prediction in organization. Do you agree with that? And you explain me? Like, monthly pay, compared with traditional one on hidden cost.
E: It is very easy to estimate, because each license to each customers.
I1: license in person and it depend on how many people in the system?
E: yes, for example, 10 persons, it means 10 licenses in the CRM system. No extra cost, nothing cost on top. Only cost is training cost and consultant cost, so, it is very easy to estimate how much it going to cost.

I1: what if you customer server break down, it that your responsibility to pay for that?
E: It doesn't happen.
I1: Good.

I1: SaaS can get rid of being locking in long license in vendors, compared with the traditional CRM system, do you agree with that?
E: yes, I agree.
I1: Can you explain me about that? Because you also have you contract will your customers right?
E: It like, when you have mobile phone. You also have contract with provider in some term (start with one year contract) and it cost you monthly, not in log term. CRM on-demand is just like that.

I1: Next one is, did SaaS play the important role to improve deployment and management in CRM system?
E: Here, in this point. One is not better that other one when it comes to management. I don't see any benefits in this point in SaaS as manager.

I1: Did SaaS improve the implementation speed?
E: definitely
I1: How different?
E: It is very different.
I1: Mostly, how long does it take in approximately for whole process.
E: Ahh… one part of our company, 4 persons, it take about half a year, to finish whole of the process. But sometime it depends on how complicate of the system too.

I1: As we know that, it can free up internal resource, you don't need to have you r own IT resource. Do you agree with that?
E: Of course, like I explain at the beginning, all is in vendors.

I1: SaaS improve the mobility, you can work anywhere that can access to the internet. Do you agree with that?
E: Yes, I agree.
I1: Is that any problem, I mean like because, internet might have a problem?
E: Yes, It can be the problem. System is not 100% offline, you better online.
I1: No offline?
E: Yes, we have, but it is not 100% work well.

I1: This one, it create high and fast ROI, return of investment. Do you agree?
E: It does, because the initial investment is so little. I don't know that it is high ROI or not but it fast ROI, of course.
I1: it's fast ROI. Ok, but you not sure about high.
E: yes.

I1: It more flexible to change CRM system as business circumstance is changed. It like your customer wants to change something, they just call you and you will talk care of that?
E: Well, I never have the question from customer about this. So, I might be able to answer exactly in this question. But of course,
I1: That's ok. No problem.

I1: Last benefits are, everything is taking care by vendors, and you don't have to do anything.
E: well, couple of reasons, of course, having vendor the taking care for CRM system is good. Another one, where does the CRM system get data from, the external data, I don't have to think about that if I have the web-based, because vendor will take care for that. And secured that we work together, we are reliable and also.
I1: As you are vendors, it not only customers that get benefits from this, also vendors too.
E: Yes.

I1: So, Let's begin with Drawback of SaaS. As you know that the very popular problem, most of customer concern about security, can you explain me about that? How? Do you have any mention to explain to your customers about this issue?
E: The main reason is that, example, all information is belong to customers, I don't have right to use it. Of course, I might mistake and use it, but they will sue me as against of the contract in security issue.
I1: very time that your customers come to you, did they always concern about this problem.
E: no, they don't.

I1: Another big problem is integration, as you know that your customers might not have only CRM system, they might want to integrate their system into your CRM system. Are there any problem? Can u explain me?
E: As my experience, it not problem with Microsoft platform, but when it comes to another system, getting more complicated and then we ask customer, we can adapt it but it will cause a lot of money. Our preference is to change into Microsoft platform data, and it will work very well with that.
I1: Did you ever found customers ask you a real time integration system?
E: no.

I1: Next, most of customer concern about configuration and customization. Most of people understand that understand that CRM on-demand have less flexibility to change or adapt the application to suit their business process. Do you agree with this? Do you have any solution for them?
E: First of all, I will ask customer, how important is it, because the most cases is not that important to do configuration.
I1: U mean if you can avoid this you will, but if not, what you going to do?
E: when it comes to more complicated, it will cause a lot of money. Our system is cover 80% of demand in most business process. I think it enough.
I1: So, can we say like traditional is better in this issue.
E: Yes, but on top of that it depend on culture of working too.

I1: Next one is, in control of application and data; customer will lose the control of their application and data. DO you agree with that?
E: No, this one I'm not agreeing with that. They own their application and information.

I1: What about reliability and connectivity, Did you have the problem with that, I mean your customers.

E: Not so much.
I1: So, you don't think that it is not the disadvantage of CRM on-demand
E: Yes, and now, most of CRM system is held in internet too. I don't see any different.

I1: yeah, and I told you that customers wonder about vendors lock-in and long term commitment. But this one you already answer me, you will have only short contract and if they want, they can continue the contract. What if, your customer not happy with your system, can they cancel it, and you will give their data back to them?
E: Ahh… Yes.
I1: From your vendors' point of view, did you lose anything from this situation?
E: of course, I don't want to lose customers. I need to listen to customer all the time and make them happy.

I1: What about lack of flexibility, offering, functionality? Do you agree with this?
E: If you going to use the CRM system is no, but if you going to use ERP system then yes. Cause, depend on which information do you need. When I talking to CRM system, the information and data is not that much to handle, but comparing with the produce system, it is the hard job to do it.
I1: So, you don't think this is disadvantage?
E: Ahh… yes.

I1: As you known that, SaaS can help in implementation very fast, less money, less afford, so, it can create reduction of CRM benefits in its own system. Do you agree with that?
E: This question connects to the question before, I can agree with this. If I working in back office, then I'm not sure that SaaS can help to improve my work or not.

I1: And the last one, culture different, SaaS will provide the new way of working? Do you think it can cause the problem?
E: The other you have before, it focusing on technique stuff, but here is totally different from here.
I1: I understand that.
E: But you ask that how we can keep motivation, as manager how can I manage employee and how can I share knowledge in organization.
E: I don't see the connection between system and behavior of people. Those two things are separated. But in some say, it might relate to each other.

I2: When you going to see customers, do you want customers to prepare or expect anything to make your system work more efficient?
E: Only thing I expect from customer is skill to using computer of each customer.

I2: What point that you concern in benefits and drawbacks?
E: Fast implementation, Fast ROI. With drawbacks, I'm not sure about, security, vendor lock-in, and lack of flexibility, low CRM benefits, and Cultural different.

Logica Ltd.
Interviewer1: Thanawin Ratametha **(I1)**
Interviewer2: Manasa Veeragandham **(I2)**
Interviewee: Johan Johansson **(E)**

I1: Can you introduce your self and your job description?
E: More or less analysis and developer and working with different kind of CRM system from the time he starts to working. Now is project manager. Now I'm working with CRM on-demand which is quite new and we focus only this. Microsoft Dynamic.
I1: You are provider?
E: Yes

I1: How can your CRM system help your customer?
E: We working like consultant firm, we don't sale pre-define package, we sale package out the box and we customize it what customer need. Microsoft CRM solution that comes in the package, the benefit of CRM on-demand system is everything is in one page. How much money they can save. But it depend on how much technique their require too.
I1: You provide only on-demand
E: I not sure that we provide or on-demand.

I1: So, I will begin asking about the benefits. First one, SaaS can reduce cost of the price, TCO of CRM system.
E: it is a bit hard to say yes or no. It's depend, if you customer need a lot of integration, so it not good for them. But they have good system and integration system to serve them, so it yes.

I1: Next, SaaS reduce up-front and IT initial.
E: Yes, of course, if you don't have to buy the service.
I1: Any effect to implementation process.
E: Depend of what kind of system their run. Some companies not ready for on-demand, but some is already started. CRM system is quite fast to implement if you need only CRM system, but the problem is integration and link to other system.
(Less than a week)

I1: Low implementation and investment risk.
E: No, h/w but mostly not h/w that is the problem. But integration with other system is the problem, otherwise yes!!! Not major factor. In h/w is yes, but in total cost, risk still there. Not sure, not major factor

I1: cost prediction
E: I'm not sure. I'm not seeing any different between on-demand and on-premise. But up-front at the beginning is might be less money, but in long term is same. I'm sure that it's benefit.
I1: What about hidden cost?
E: No, it cost something every month. You don't know what price going to come.

I1: get rid of lock-in into long license.
E: Yes, you can change every time you want.
I1: But also have some contract.
E: Yes, but not long

I1: What about ease of deployment and management?

E: May be, small and less complex, you will get benefits in on-demand, but if they have existing system, the work is same. On-premise is much longer implementation process, but due to the complicate of the system.

I1: What about improvement in implementation speed?
E: Yes

I1: No need IT infra structure, and can focusing on core business
E: I'm agreeing, you don't need IT to take care server, but still need some IT staff (IT helpdesk). Also key user, it they can't solve it, they will come to us.

I1: It can improve mobility?
E: Yes, if you can use internet with IE, you can access to the system.
I1: Can you work offline?
E: No

I1: Also, high and fast return of investment?
E: Yes and No, due to the complex of the system and business. It is not different between on-premise and on-demand except h/w and license.

I1: Flexibility to change the CRM application as their business commitments circumstance is change
E: I'm not agreeing with that, it is same as on-premise system. I mean the way we have to work.

I1: Responsibility is on vendor, it is one of benefit, do you agree with this?.
E: I'm not agree, customers should see vendors more often, because they need strong project group. So, this is not a benefit for on-demand, in opposite way, it might cause some problem.

I2: Which is strongest benefit do you think?
E: It is very easy for small companies that no need to have new server.

I1: Everybody concerning about security issue?
E: Yes, definitely.
I1: How can you handle this problem?
E: We need to explain the security issue to those customers, and on-premise system also have security problem too. But I'm agreeing that security is drawbacks.

I1: What about the integration problem?
E: Yes, definitely the drawback. This is main drawback of Saleforce.com.
I1: Do you ever face this problem during implementation?
E: They try to avoid this problem, but mostly if they need more integration, they will not choose the on-demand.
I1: What about customization and configuration problem in SaaS compared with traditional system?
E: Normally, SaaS version of the problem, don't' come in full package, you can do much more on SaaS compared with on-premise. But I'm agreeing that it is one of the drawbacks.

I1: also with the controllability of application and data, some customers might feel that they lose the control of application and data?
E: I think it is same thing as security, it is only on their feeling, they might feel that it not in their control but actually it is. And also this kind of technology is still young, might be it need time to people get use to it. In few year, all system will be on-demand.

I1: reliability and connectivity, most of customer, they have some doubt because of they need internet connect to access to their CRM system.
E: I don't think it is the problem. But it still the drawback (not important), Most companies have secure internet connection, and CRM business process is not that complicated, when system is down, it will not effect to the main business process. Not agree.

I1: Customers worries about vendor lock-in and long term commitment. Do you agree with that?
E: I don't think it is a problem, there is no different between both systems. No matter what the process still same such as migration.

I1: Do you think the problem of lack of flexibility, offering, features and functionality are SaaS weakness?
E: Yes, I'm agreeing on that. They have a lot of features but compared with on-premise, on-premise is better. On-premise is the classic one, if they need safe in their system, they will choose on-demand.

I1: SaaS will cause reduction in CRM benefits itself.
E: I'm partly agree, if you lose some functionality, you also lose CRM benefit. But SaaS is more and more complete, in few year, it will same as on-premise.

I1: and the one drawback, the culture different, as on-demand, employee can change the way their work. Do you think this is the problem?
E: I think there are a lot of concerns in this area. SaaS is good for young people and new modern company.

I2: As from traditional to on-demand, Are they any different between these system, what kind of benefit could they carry from that?
E: The traditional one is crap, and the new on-demand system is very good.

I2: is that taking a lot of time to implement?
E: it is very fast to implement, out of the box, but it depend on type of business process too.

I2: What is the strongest drawback that you want to change?
E: I think, the standard integration system should be change, for example, Microsoft should provide the integration platform to the partner, and it would be perfect and useful for implementer.

I2: What do you expect from your customers?
E: They should come up with the idea how to use the system and willingness to use the CRM system without against the system.

I1: Do you also providing train program for your user?
E: Yes, of course.
I2: Is that system is cheaper than other system?
E: Yes, compared with ERP or BI system, CRM is much cheaper than those systems and easy to implement too.

CenturioCRM Ltd.
Interviewer1: Thanawin Ratametha **(I1)**
Interviewer2: Manasa Veeragandham **(I2)**
Interviewee: Michael Duffy **(E)**

I1: Our research is doing the research about CRM as a Service. As we know that CRM as a Service is CRM system that apply the SaaS platform into CRM system. And their have it own benefit and drawback. So, our research tries to evaluate the benefits and drawback. We got key benefits and drawbacks from previous research in last few years. And our research question will based on this research model.

I1: So, the first one as we know SaaS can reduce the cost and price, I mean total cost of ownership of CRM system. Do you agree with this?
E: Yes!

I1: Ok and it also can reduce the upfront cost and IT initial cost during the implementation, you also agree with this? I mean at the beginning when your customer try to create CRM system, SaaS can reduce the initial cost of implementation process.
E: The problem is when compared with the traditional CRM, when you doing the price calculation in software as a service, you buy the service when everything is included, including the platform infrastructure. When you calculating investment of CRM, they need to add service and all infrastructure and some companies, they not calculate it as the back hidden cost. So when you do evaluate between software as a service and tradition system, you need also calculate the cost of those infrastructure.

I1: and the next one is, SaaS claim that it can low implementation and investment risk. Do you agree with that?
E: Yeah.

I2: Does it help in cost prediction for the organization?
E: the good thing of SaaS is organization that buys it, they know exactly cost at the base, and there are no surprises. And it is very important factor.

I1: Yes, and also SaaS can get rid of being locked into the long license from the vendor compared with the traditional CRM system.
E: No, we are open.
I1: So, you don't have a long term contract with your customers?
E: Definitely, yes, we have a long term relationship with our customers, but we not lock up the client.
I1: So, mostly you have annual contract, I mean year by year contract.
E: Yes.

I1: Also, SaaS play important role to improve the deployment and management in CRM system.
E: Yeah, that's true.
I1: Also including the upgrading the server, software and so on.
E: Everything is included.
I1: For example, if you have to upgrading your customer server, did you charge your customer in this cost?
E: No.

I1: Compared with traditional CRM system, on-demand system can improve the implementation speed, do you agree?
E: Yes.
I1: How different?
E: could be very different, depend on cost of project.
I1: ok

I1: And some people said that if you implementing CRM on-demand your organization don't need to have your own IT infrastructure and it can free up internal resource in the organization.
E: the most important factor in organization is the triangle which where you have the IT staff here, you have IT manager here and you have top management here on the top. When you selling the software as a service solution, you can go directly to the top and do everything with them, you don't have talk with the leave parts. Which mean that of course, their internal IT people see acknowledge fear because if they investing the software as a service, they will not have any opt. That will eliminate the time and money.

I2: Did SaaS improve the mobility aspect in CRM on-demand?
E: yes, as so, SaaS is the internet web-based solution, everything is access in the mobile, if the mobile have the web browser.

I1: Did SaaS create high and fast ROI?
E: Definitely, yes.

I2: And SaaS allow more flexibility to change the commitment as the business circumstance is changed.
E: Yes, you have much flexibility to do the change in SaaS environment compared with the traditional system. Because SaaS solution is build on modern technology which is web-based, so you have more possibility with role management and term management than most system had. And you can do the change in few minutes where in few month in traditional system. And this is important factors.

I2: So, it is completely, vendor's responsibility in everything, and they taking care for everything for customers.
E: in term of delivery SaaS, it is important that the vendors have the normal knowledge and technical evaluate, how to delivery CRM. CRM is not software, CRM is the process. Where you need to adopt the process, how company will work, and then you have customer relationship management. Because 8 of 10 CRM project are lacking due to they are not using completely business process with you. They don't train user how to use the system. And they are lack of documentation.

I2: So, you not agree with that, this should be drawback.
E: Yeah.

I2: You think security can be issue in CRM on-demand?
E: I will ask opposite question, what security do you have?
I2: Oh.
E: So, we client are asking how good security do you have. You should reverse the question said what security do you have in your organization. Because our security is equal to the bank and our service need to be available all 24hrs and all year. And our customer have separated and different database system. And data in there is encrypted, we not allow seeing or using those data.
I1: So, you don't think this is a drawback at all?
E: not at all

I1: and also the integration problem, because most of customer, they have a lot of system, and when they implementing CRM on-demand, they might want to integrate your system with their legacy system. Do you think this is problem?
E: Not if you have the open source to integrate them, some of SaaS are quite locked in, it mean that it could be quite difficult to exchange data. But if you a clear and open interface to exchange the data such as web-service, it should be more easy to connect and exchange the data in this solution. So, our solution will use third party software to create the integration platform. So, this is the main benefits of SaaS when we applying third party software for integration compared with traditional system, it will cost a lot of money.

I2: most of customer concern about customization and configuration on CRM on-demand, do you agree with that?
E: No, again, come to the big problem, when customers try to implement something, they not do the business with you. That's why, they are lacking. So, at the beginning, we make sure that we have the right designed system in blueprint and then come to the developing process of the system and then so on. But for traditional system, it can take up to 18 months.
I1: Can I ask you about product? You providing CRM on-demand and every time that your customers come, do you have any template? Or some ready to use platform? Or you just re-build the entire thing?
E: Totally re-build the entire system
I1: So, you not like Saleforce?
E: I know Saleforce platform and lack of those platforms, that's why, I would like to get rid of those problems.

I1: Most of customers, they feel like they will lose controllability of their application and data, do you think so? When they hosting the application and data with you?
E: why? Because they do the same thing with the traditional one.
I1: Then, for example, some organizations have their own IT staffs, and they can take care their own application.
E: But they don't have expert who know well about CRM system.
I1: Oh, ok.

I1: According to CRM on-demand, they need internet to access the system, so most of customers have doubt on connectivity and reliability through the internet browser. Do you think so, and do you face this problem?
E: no, most people have internet today, even, if they don't have it in home, they also have in their mobile, so the only thing you need is browser with internet connection. And in the next 3 years, everything will be in cloud computing, you will see everything is on-demand, everything will deliver over the browser.

I1: Next one, vendor lock-in and vendor commitment.
E: No, I think, customer they see advantages of that (SaaS), But not with Saleforce, they have vendor lock-in with their customers. Because, they have very unfair contract, which mean that their customers can only upgrade but can't downgrade the contract in term of more life license. I think good license should match with gravity of company.

I1: So, you will said like your product are more flexible and you offer a lot
E: we offer from our vendors' perspective, we offer something that advantage for the client. Saleforce are the biggest customers-based, and they start the on-demand business bone, they have more or less one of the best system on the market in term of functionality, flexibility, and security and trust but they are expensive. So, the drawback is price.

I1: What about the culture different problem in CRM on-demand worker.
E: I will not said that it cause the problem in work, people that are use to work with the internet, they adopt very quick.

I2: Are there any change from traditional one to on-demand in CRM benefits?
E: Scalability and flexibility
I2: What is you strongest benefits?
E: High and Fast ROI.

I2: Anything you want to ask your customers?
E: CRM is the service; adopt your business at a time. Keep it update to get good system.

Appendix C: Survey questionnaire

C.1: www.surveygizmo.com

SurveyGizmo is the main product of Widgix, LLC, co-founded by Christian Vanek and Scott McDaniel in 2006. SurveyGizmo is an online survey software tool for designing online surveys, collecting data and performing analysis. Their tool supports a variety of online data collection methods including online surveys, online quizzes, questionnaires, web forms, and landing pages.

They designed SurveyGizmo for market research, job applications, marketing campaigns, blogs, landing pages, contact forms, sales tracking, and lead generation. Widgix, LLC and SurveyGizmo show continuous growth — even in this depressed economy. They are currently 'home' for 10 employees based in Boulder, CO. (*History and Definition of website cited from: http://www.surveygizmo.com/company/about/*) for more information please visit website below.

Website: www.surveygizmo.com

C.2: Online survey Question
Screenshot of Online survey questionnaire

CRM on-demand: its benefits and drawbacks

Lund University

Dear Sir/Madam,

We are master students in Lund University (Lund, Sweden, http://www.ics.lu.se/) in major of Information system. We are doing our Thesis research on "CRM on-demand: its benefits and drawbacks" in the supervision of Associate professor Erik Wallin (erik.wallin@ics.lu.se, phone: 046-2228027). We would like to ask your valuable time to complete our online survey about SaaS's benefits and drawbacks.

Please note that, result of survey will be used in our research for analyzing and to conclude for the valuable knowledge. If you would like to see online survey result, please contact us via email (below) and indicate your name and email. We will contact you back with result of this online survey after this survey finish.

Thank you for your time,

Thanawin Ratametha
Email: Thanawin.Ratametha@hermes.ics.lu.se

CRM on-demand: its benefits and drawbacks
What's the strength of your staff in your organization?
- Less than 10
- 10-20

- 20-50
- 50-150
- More than 150

Your organization is
- CRM system provider
- CRM system user

What type of CRM system you in your organization?
- Normal CRM (On-premise CRM)
- On-demand CRM

For On-premise CRM user/provider

Do you have plans to change from on-premise CRM to on-demand CRM system?
- Yes
- No

Please use your knowledge about on-demand CRM to answer following question about Benefits and Drawbacks of on-demand CRM (comparing with your on-premise CRM system)

For On-demand CRM user/provider

Did you implement on-premise CRM before you changed to on-demand CRM?
- Yes
- No

In case that you used to implement on-premise CRM system, please answer following question based on comparison with your old on-premise CRM system.

For On-demand and On-premise CRM user/provider

Based on our research key benefits of SaaS that effect to CRM system, please rank the rate for each Benefit as following: **(1 for strongly disagree to 5 for strongly agree)**

Benefits of SaaS

SaaS can reduce the cost and price (Total cost of ownership) during the implementation. Do you agree?
    1   2   3   4   5

SaaS can reduce up-front costs and IT initial costs. Do you agree?
    1   2   3   4   5

SaaS reduce implementation risk and investment risk. Do you agree?
    1   2   3   4   5

SaaS create clear cost prediction during implementation period. Do you agree?

1   2   3   4   5

SaaS can get rid of locked into long license in vendor. Do you agree?
1   2   3   4   5

SaaS can provide ease of deployment and management (Software/Hardware Upgrade and Maintenance). Do you agree?
1   2   3   4   5

SaaS can offer fast and quick implementation. Do you agree?
1   2   3   4   5

SaaS implementations don't need IT infrastructure and can free up internal resource in organization. Do you agree?
1   2   3   4   5

SaaS offer accessibility from everywhere (mobility in use). Do you agree?
1   2   3   4   5

SaaS offer high and fast return of investment (ROI) compared with CRM on-premise. Do you agree?
1   2   3   4   5

SaaS offer flexibility to change usage commitments as business circumstances change. Do you agree?
1   2   3   4   5

SaaS can free customer work by put all responsibility to providers (Providers will take care for everything). Do you agree?
1   2   3   4   5

Please rank the most important SaaS's benefits you think that will affect your CRM system:
    1. Low cost and price (Total cost of ownership)
    2. Low up-front costs and IT initial costs
    3. Low implementation and investment risk
    4. Clear cost prediction
    5. Not locked into long license
    6. Ease of deployment and management
    7. Fast implementation
    8. No need IT infrastructure and free up internal resource
    9. Mobility
    10. High and fast ROI
    11. Flexibility to change usage commitments
    12. Responsibility is on the vendor

Based on our research key drawbacks of SaaS that effect to CRM system, please rank the rate for each Drawback as following: (**1 for strongly disagree to 5 for strongly agree**)

Drawbacks of SaaS

SaaS cause security problems in data and application. Do you agree?
    1   2   3   4   5

SaaS cause integration problems with legacy system. Do you agree?
    1   2   3   4   5

SaaS make low customization and configuration of CRM application. Do you agree?
    1   2   3   4   5

SaaS is lack of controllability in application and data. Do you agree?
    1   2   3   4   5

SaaS make low reliability and connectivity such as internet goes down. Do you agree?
    1   2   3   4   5

SaaS has vendor lock-in problem and long-term vendor commitment problem (can't change CRM provider during the contrast). Do you agree?
    1   2   3   4   5

SaaS is lack of flexibility, offering, features and functionality in CRM application. Do you agree?
    1   2   3   4   5

SaaS reduces CRM benefits, because of standard in CRM application and lack of functionality. Do you agree?

    1   2   3   4   5

SaaS can cause cultural difference such as Employee work from home. Do you agree?
    1   2   3   4   5

Please rank the most important SaaS's drawbacks that you think will affect your CRM system:
    1. Security
    2. Integration
    3. Customization and configuration
    4. Control of application and data
    5. Reliability and connectivity
    6. Vendor lock-in and long term vendor commitment
    7. Lack of flexibility, offering, features and functionality
    8. Low CRM benefits
    9. Culture different

In your opinion, Comparing on-demand CRM and on-premise CRM system, which one is your champion?
    On-premise CRM
    On-demand CRM
    Depend on type of usage

Please explain: _____

References

Adebanjo, D. (2008). e-crm Implementation: a comparison of three approaches. *International Conference on Management of Innovation and Technology*, 457-462.

Anderson, R. D., Sweeney, J. D., William, A. T., Freeman, J., & Shoesmith, E. (2007). *Statistics for Business and Economics Book*. London: Thomas Learning.

Anthes, G. (2009). SaaS Realities. *Computerworld*, 43, 1, 21.

Biddick, M. (2008). Time For A Walk In The Cloud. *InformationWeek*, 1208, 40.

Borck, R. J. (2005). CRM on Demand. *InfoWorld*, 27, 2, 30.

Brown, S. A. (2000). *Customer Relationship Management - A Strategic Imperative in the World of eBusiness*. Canada: John Wiley & Sons Ltd.

Campbell, A. (2008*). Cloud Computing - Get Used to the Term, The App Gap*, Retrieved April, 20th 2009 [online] http://www.theappgap.com/cloud-computing-get-used-to-the-term.html.

Camponovo, G., Pigneur, Y., Rangone, A., & Renga, F. (2005). Mobile customer relationship management: an explorative investigation of the Italian consumer market. *International Conference on Mobile Business,* 42-48.

Chenail, J. R. (1995). Presenting Qualitative Data. *The Qualitative Report*, 2, 3.

Chou, W. (2008). Web Services: Software-as-a-Service (SaaS), Communication, and Beyond. *Congress on Services*, 23, 1.

David, K. (2000). CRM: Who ya gonna call?. *Business Communications Review*, 30, 12, 52-56.

Denscombe, M. (2007). *The good research guide: for small-scale social research projects* (3th ed.). McGraw-Hill International: Open University Press.

Dubie, D. (2005). Pay-as-you-go pricing picks up. *Network World*, 22, 30, 48.

Finch, C. (2006). The Benefits of the Software-as-a-Service Model. *Employee Benefit Plan Review*, 60, 8, 25.

Fred, B. (2009). Cloud computing. *CA Magazine*, 142, 2, 44-46.

Fonseca, B. (2008). SaaS Benefits Starting to Outweigh Risks. *Computerworld*, 42, 19, 12.

Gartner report (2008). Gartner Says Cloud Computing Will Be As Influential As E-business. *Special Report Examines the Realities and Risks of Cloud Computing*, Stamford, June 26, 2008.

Google Docs. Retrieved May, 1st 2009 [online] http://www.google.com/google-d-s/tour1.html

Gordjin, J., & Akkermans, H. (2001). Designing and Evaluating E-Business Models. *Intelligent Systems*, 14, 7, 11-17.

Gruman, G., & Knorr, E. (2008). What cloud computing really means. *InfoWorld*. Retrieved May, 23rd 2009 [online] http://www.infoworld.com/article/08/04/07/15FE-cloud-computing-reality 1.html.

Hall, E. M. (2009). SaaS Surprises. *Computerworld*, 43, 12, 18.

Hedman, J., & Kalling, T. (2003). The Business model concept: theoretical underpinnings and empirical illustrations. *European Journal of Information Systems*, 12, 49-59.

Hewitt, M. (2008). APPS ON TAP. *Management Today*, 60.

Hichem, A., & Wahiba M. (2005). E-Business: Modeling and Opportunities. *Proceedings of International E-Business Conference*, June 23-25, Tunisia.

InformationWeek report. *A Walk In The Clouds: Cloud Computing Analytics Report*. InformationWeek Analytics.

Israel, M., & Hay, L. (2006). *Research Ethics for Social Scientists*. London: SAGE Publications.

Johnson, K. L. (2002). New Views on Digital CRM. *Sloan Management Review fall*, 2002.

Jonas, H., & Thomas, K. (2002). *IT and Business Models Book*. Sweden: Daleke Grafiska AB.

Judith, L. (2009). SaaS: flexible, efficient & affordable. *KM World*, 18, 1, 10-11.

Jukic, N., Jukic, B., Meamber, A. L., & Nezlek, G. (2003). Implementing Polyinstantiation as a Strategy for Electronic Commerce Customer Relationship Mangement. *International Journal of Electronic Commerce*, 7, 2, 10.

Kabiraj, S. (2003). Electronic customer relationship management: origin and opportunities. *Engineering Management Conference*, 482-486.

Kvale, S. (1996). *Interviews: An Introduction to Qualitative Research Interviewing*. London: SAGE publications.

Lager, M. (2009). The Shots Heard Round the World. *Customer relationship management*, 13, 1, 16-17.

Lashar, D. J. (2008). The Hidden Cost of SaaS. *Customer Relationship Management*, 12, 5, 14.

Ledford, J. (2004). Reducing CRM's Total Cost of Ownership. *Customer Relationship Management*, 8, 8, 15.

Likert, R. (1932). A Technique for the Measurement of Attitudes. *Archives of Psychology*, 140, 1–55.

Lincoln, Y. S. (1995). Emerging criteria for quality in qualitative and interpretive research. *Qualitative Inquiry*, 1, 275-289.

Madsen, J. J. (2009). The Pros and Cons of SaaS. *Buildings*, 103, 3, 26.

Martin, M. H. (1998). An ERP Strategy. *Fortune*, 95-97.

Matt, W. (2008). The Sales Force Software Shift. *Pharmaceutical Executive*, 28, 9, 128.

Muther, A. (2002), *Customer Relationship Management: Electronic Customer Care in the New Economy*. Springer.

Oates, B. J. (2006). *Researching Information Systems and Computing*. London: Sage Publications.

Patton, M. Q. (1990). *Qualitative Evaluation and Research Methods* (2nd ed.). Newbury Park, CA: Sage Publications.

Payne, A., Christopher, M., Clark, M., & Peck, H. (1998). *Relationship Marketing for Competitive Advantage Winning and Keeping Customers*. Butterworth Heinemann: Oxford.

Preston, R. (2008). Customers Fire A Few Shots At Cloud Computing. *InformationWeek*, 1191, 52.

Pring, B. (2005). Adoption of Software as a Service Is Happening Outside of CRM. *Gartner Report*, Dec16, 2005

Qualitative Validity, from Research Methods Knowledge Base, Retrieved April, 21st 2009 [Online] http://www.socialresearchmethods.net/kb/qualval.php

Reid, K. C. (2009). SaaS: The secret weapon for profits (and the planet). *EContent*, 32, 1, 24-29.

Scanlon, H. J., & Wieners, B. (1999). *The Internet Cloud*, Retrieved April, 19th 2009 [online] http://www.thestandard.com/article/0,1902,5466,00.html.

Software & Information Industry Association [SIIA] (2004). *Software as a Service: Changing the paradigm in the software industry*, July 2004.

Stimpson, J. (2008). The Move to Hosted Applications. *The Practical Accountant*, 41, 2, 25.

Wei, S., Zhang, X., Guo, J. C., Sun, P., & Su, H. (2008). *Software as a Service: Configuration and Customization Perspectives*, 2008.

Weier, H. M. (2008a). SaaS Integration: Real-World Problems, And How CIOs Are Solving Them. *InformationWeek*, October 20, 2008.

Weier, H. M. (2008b). The Real Test Of CRM As A Service. *InformationWeek*, 1168, 28.

Weier, H. M. (2009). CRM As A Service Offered In New Options. *InformationWeek*, 1219, 16.

Weier, H. M., & Smith, L. (2007). Serious About SaaS. *InformationWeek*, 1134, 46.

Williams, J. M., & Sears, C. (2008). Who Coined the Phrase Cloud Computing?, Retrieved April, 23rd 2009 [online] http://www.johnmwillis.com/cloud-computing/who-coined-the-phrase-cloud-computing/.

Wind, J., & Mahajan, V. (2002). *Convergence Marketing: Strategies for Reading the New Hybrid Consumer.* Prentice-Hall, Englewood Cliffs: FT press.

Winer, S. R. (2001). A Framework for Customer Relationship Management. *California Management Review*, 43, 4.

Yin, K. R. (2003). *Case study research: Design and Methods* (3rd ed.). London: SAGE publications.

VDM publishing house ltd.

Scientific Publishing House
offers
free of charge publication
of current academic research papers, Bachelor's Theses, Master's Theses, Dissertations or Scientific Monographs

If you have written a thesis which satisfies high content as well as formal demands, and you are interested in a remunerated publication of your work, please send an e-mail with some initial information about yourself and your work to *info@vdm-publishing-house.com*.

Our editorial office will get in touch with you shortly.

VDM Publishing House Ltd.
Meldrum Court 17.
Beau Bassin
Mauritius
www.vdm-publishing-house.com

VDM Verlag Dr. Müller   LAP LAMBERT Academic Publishing   SVH Südwestdeutscher Verlag für Hochschulschriften

Printed in Germany by
Amazon Distribution
GmbH, Leipzig